WHY SELL
TACOS
IN
AFRICA

WHY SELL
TACOS
IN
AFRICA

Building a Business Through
Change and Uncertainty

PAUL OBERSCHNEIDER

LegacyPRESS

TABLE OF CONTENTS

THE NEW NORMAL 1

Preface 4

Introduction 8

Chapter 1: THE IMPORTANCE OF CHANCE MEETINGS . . 12

Chapter 2: IMPRESSIONS 23

Chapter 3: BELIEVING 31

Chapter 4: SURRENDER TO WIN 39

Chapter 5: REBOOT 44

Chapter 6: THE NARRATIVE 51

Chapter 7: HELP IS FOR THE ASKING 57

Chapter 8: GREAT TEAMS BUILD BUSINESSES 64

Chapter 9: THE LEADERSHIP MYTH 71

Chapter 10: THE IDEA MYTH 77

Chapter 11: GET GOOD AT EXECUTION 84

Chapter 12: FRIENDS AND TURKEY DINNERS 92

Chapter 13: KNOW THE NUMBERS 101

Chapter 14: BUILDING A BRAND 107

Chapter 15: THE IMPORTANCE OF BASKETS 114

Chapter 16: WINNING AND LOSING 119

Chapter 17: IT'S ALWAYS DARKEST BEFORE DAWN . . . 126

Chapter 18: LIFE AFTER EXIT 131

Chapter 19: SELLING TACOS IN AFRICA 137

Acknowledgements 145

About the Author 147

THE NEW NORMAL

AS I WRITE THIS, we are experiencing an unprecedented time in our lives that appeared in the form of a virus. The result of this global pandemic has nearly shutdown the global economy to levels not seen since the Great Depression and will certainly have long lasting effects on the way we live and do things.

We are seeing jobs being lost, businesses being shut down, and the vast majority of people don't really know how they will manage when things start to shift back to normality. But one thing is for sure—it will pass.

When starting out any new business, you just never know how things are going to pan out ultimately, or how you will need to pivot as the market changes. But start you must, and you keep going; making changes as you go along until step-by-step you stumble across a formula that works. But even that formula will change over time. Business, like life, is ever changing, and adaptation is the key to survival and success.

Looking ahead, the effects of the Covid-19 virus will change the way we interact with each other, and how we do things. I think it has already shown us that as humans we are a resilient bunch, and we tend to come together in support of one another in times of great market dislocations and uncertainty. And terrible as this current situation has been, it has given us all time to pause and reflect and think about the important things in life and how we see ourselves in the bigger picture. At least, that's what it's done for me. The "important" things have become less so, and the seemingly unimportant things have become the more important.

Two years ago I started another venture after essentially retiring at age 48. Twelve years later, I was coming back to a market and skill-set I knew but that had gotten rusty and slightly out of date with time. The salad days were over, and I was starting from scratch again, with only a short PowerPoint and one person helping me. It was just an idea at the time with a lot of questions I needed to flesh out, answer and test.

But it's in moments like that, of not knowing for certain how things will pan out, that life brings out the best in all of us. It forces us to think out of the box and reboot our thinking.

Today will produce outcomes we may never have considered before; changes will take place at an accelerated rate; new ideas will emerge and new ways of doing things will become self-evident where it may not have been so clear beforehand.

Years earlier when the Berlin Wall came down and Central and Eastern Europe was left free to manage on their own and throw back 50 years of Soviet legacy in one single moment in time, great opportunities suddenly emerged that weren't there before. At the time, it wasn't so clear, but as a huge market dislocation appeared, many people were placed to help make changes happen. Those early participants, like myself, had no clue what the future looked like, but we did what we could and found ways to make things better, thereby benefiting our communities, our working places, and of course in the end ourselves as early entrants.

I would like to think that while this global pandemic has wreaked havoc on the lives of many, that there will be opportunities to make better choices and to make changes that we can all benefit from. For some, that will mean poking a hole through the old in order to push through into new technologies, systems, and ways to improve things generally.

I know for me, building something new is always exciting. Pulling new people together, trying stuff on, seeing what works and what doesn't, and solving problems is an exciting, creative process.

The point is that some things will change forever, and dislocations in markets like this create opportunities; uncontested markets, and windows of opportunity to make things better than they were. Stepping back and having a look at how you are currently doing things and the willingness to create those changes are the first steps to providing a huge new service or new product that is truly useful for everyone. That's really the magic of building anything no matter what the circumstances may be.

PREFACE

THE TITLE OF THIS BOOK might make you think it's about doing business in Africa. It's not.

Then again, maybe it is. But really that's not how it started.

The title helps explain how I built a business from scratch almost by accident in the post-Soviet era from 1992 to 2008. I started the business from nothing, in a country totally unfamiliar to me. I ended up building one of the largest cross-border property companies across the emerging market of Central and Eastern Europe. Every step was filled with loads of uncertainty and changing market conditions and challenges; fortunately, I was backed by a rising tide of global liquidity and of course, the help of great people along the way.

The title is a metaphor for finding opportunities and building businesses in markets where there is rampant uncertainty, and a willingness to go where the shifting tides carry you. This could be true of any new market, or where markets, like today, are changing as never before. Fundamentally, it's also about learning to let go while staying in control of events and opportunities.

It's hard to find tacos in Africa, which means if you start a Mexican restaurant in Ghana or Nigeria, you probably won't face the same stiff competition you'd find in Los Angeles or London.

This book is about a journey most people don't choose to take. People play it safe, they hate risk, and are fearful. They may think they want the adventure; they talk about the adventure, but when push comes to shove, they feel more comfortable in the familiar. Anything outside the status quo freaks people out. Most want approval and permission from others, they want support, they even play the victim when things go wrong. Rather than digging deep and developing unshakeable faith and climbing that mountain of worry and seemingly insurmountable obstacles, they opt for the same.

Doing something different and stretching yourself is hard, especially when in uncharted territory. From the time we were kids, we've learned how to survive and maintain the familiar. So we end up doing the familiar all the time. We follow a well-trodden path and script, and yet are surprised when the results are mediocre at best.

But playing that same movie over and over can get real boring. The sad part is that many would-be entrepreneurs who don't take the journey will end up with the chronic pain of knowing that beyond their backyard there is another world of stuff to do and to be done and they missed the boat.

So the adventure calls.

The good news is that you don't need a 5-year business plan to begin your journey; you don't need to know all the answers. All you need is the willingness to start, fall down, step in shit, get up and do it again, and have faith that tomorrow will be different. Hopefully, you will learn from your mistakes. In fact, the good stuff happens when you're busy and not looking.

Building a business is an epic journey and behind every great journey is an epic story. These are the journeys most of us never hear about. The endless hours of slogging it out, the hundreds of "no's", trying to pay the bills with hardly any or no income; It goes on and on, until you just want someone to shoot you.

Instead, today most of what we are fed and buy into is the social media hype of get-rich-quick schemes and overnight success stories that savvy marketers pawn off on us as real. Some of them are pretty darn convincing. We are bombarded every day by fast news and glamorous marketing, which screws up our thinking because we can't differentiate between what's true and what's not. We don't have time to think and be who we are really meant to be because we are constantly being bombarded by more information. We are forever chasing shadows created by other people.

The "real-deal" kind of success comes with a price tag; it's hard, comes slow, and requires presence every day until at some point you figure out exactly the right thing to do. Small steps, almost unnoticeable until a quantum moment arrives which is a result of all those steps. Tides will turn against you suddenly, and then you figure things out. And that's when the magic really happens. Most people never get that far. It takes a bit of dumb patience and faith. You need to believe the impossible and know that success is right around the corner, whether you can see it or not.

Why Sell Tacos in Africa is about my journey and my story with a lot of my random insights and shoe leather thrown in between.

It starts with a lot of foundational background stuff, then with me leaving my past behind as a Chicago and Wall Street floor trader, and arriving in Estonia in 1992 with just $400 in savings in my blue jeans pocket. It goes on to explain how what was meant to be a short holiday, turned into almost two decades of building stuff.

I never planned it that way. I set off on a short holiday before business school and never in a million years thought about starting a business, let alone a super successful one.

Real life happens unexpectedly. John Lennon said it best, "Life's what happens when you're busy making other plans".

Along the way of any journey comes some painful points, which I try and explain in hindsight because, as I've come to discover, the pain of any journey is worth every minute; and I wouldn't change a thing.

INTRODUCTION

WHEN YOU SIT AROUND doing nothing, time seems as slow as Mississippi molasses dripping off an old wooden spoon. Thinking is a good thing, reading is good too, but at some point, you need to get off the sofa, stop couch surfing, down a double espresso and grab some courage and just get going, even if you have no idea where that might be.

Kind of like I did.

In 1992, my friend Roger dropped me off at Kennedy Airport in New York. It was an unusually hot April day, and the air con wasn't working in his brand new 4x4. I'd quit smoking two weeks earlier, so I was a bit on the edge, and the two deli coffees from Oscar's in Westport I'd downed earlier sure didn't help.

Roger and I had been friends for a long time. We'd met in 1987 and had been through a lot together. We were both clean and sober about five years, and had laughed, worried, and cried together that entire time. We were best buddies.

We gave each other an awkward hug at the departure drop-off and said goodbye. I told him I'd be back in a few weeks to pick up my stuff and then I'd head up to Boston to graduate school. I had one bag and $400 in my pocket, and I was off for a quick discovery trip to find my family roots. What I did not know, was that this would be a life-changing journey and I would never call him to pick me up.

For this to make sense, you need some background. Most

sensible people just don't get on a plane to Estonia and never come back.

Whether I knew at the time or not, I had chosen to walk away and start again. I don't think I was consciously making that decision, but subconsciously that is exactly what I was doing. Looking back, I never had any intention of going to business school or calling Roger. Deep down I think I knew that all along.

From 1982 to 1987, I'd traveled a pretty wild and rocky road on Wall Street. Looking back, a lot of it was fun, but most of it was sheer excess and then some. I'd done five years as a futures and options trader on the New York Futures Exchange and American Stock Exchange. I was a compulsive A type personality, running from the pain of a lot of childhood wounds and I used any excuse I could get to play hard. I was young, stupid and immortal. For me, being in New York in the 80s was like some epic party that never ended. I was taken in by everything the Big Apple could offer and I gobbled up as much as I could.

When most guys went home after a long night out, I'd just keep going. More booze, more drugs, more music. Just more. Looking back, I have no idea why I'm even still alive, given some of the places I'd end up at five in the morning. The whole thing nearly killed me. By 1987, I was burned out. Finished. To top it all off, I was broke, and I was afraid to show my face. Totally wrecked by where I had let my life end up so quickly.

When I got fired in 1987, I was a physical and mental wreck. I had no real friends; my family had disowned me, I had no remaining confidence, and to be honest, no real-life skills—I lived in a world of pretend. Yet, when I looked at myself in the mirror, I knew I was better than that. I wanted to do something meaningful with my life, I just didn't know what that was. All I knew was I was not that person. Deep down, I knew there was more. And I knew I needed to give myself a chance to find it.

By 1992, I felt I was ready to start my life and career all over again. Business school was waiting for me in September. My life plan; go on this trip, explore some family roots, hang out, come back, go to school and get a normal job. That was the Doris Day narrative I had bought into.

When Roger dropped me off at the airport that day, I was thirty-three years old, and I'd spent the last five years going to AA meetings and getting my head straight. I had to really dig deep, face my demons and get honest. And I had to learn how to reboot my life. All that rebooting requires loads of faith. Which, by the way was about all I had left in the bank.

By the time I got on that Finnair flight in New York, I was a very different person. I was open to anything, and really had nothing to lose. That is one of the best places to start from. I had been given a gift; a gift of faith that no matter what happened, everything was going to be just fine. I scrubbed up and I was headed out to meet the world as the new me.

·······

WITHIN A FEW SHORT MONTHS after leaving New York for Estonia, I'd earned $100,000 by simply writing business plans for people who couldn't write them themselves. It was a time of high adventure in a small transitioning Eastern European country. I kept that money in shoeboxes under the bed of my rented Soviet-era apartment because most of the banks had failed and I had no other place to put it all. It was more cold cash than I'd ever held at one time before. That grub stake was the start of everything that came after.

So instead of heading back home like everyone—including myself—had expected when I'd left New York, I ended up staying; thinking that I would make more money and go to business school later in the year. Of course, that never happened.

One thing leads to another, and over the next year I helped a young guy I'd met start a bank without knowing a thing about banking or credit. Over the course of the next eighteen years, I just took one step at a time and almost by accident created one of the largest real estate companies in Central and Eastern Europe—building shopping centers, residential homes, and five-star boutique hotels across the region, and just for fun, created Europe's world-famous Christmas market in Tallinn (because, selfishly, I was trying to get tourists into my hotel in the winter season!).

I was in the right place at the right time. And to top it all off, I rode a killer wave of liquidity gushing out of the US banking system which spread across Europe and over the small, wild markets of the former Soviet Union. Looking back, it was one heck of a party.

No spoilers, but confidentially, the end of my party was equally lucky and just as unplanned as showing up for it.

Chapter 1

THE IMPORTANCE OF
CHANCE MEETINGS

See things from the other person's point of view.
—Dale Carnegie

IN 1992 I MET A GUY from Finland who, believe it or not, called himself "Elvis". He cut his hair like Elvis, and even cut a record of Elvis songs. To say he was a total nutcase would be putting it mildly. Elvis was part of the expat community that I occasionally hung around with. One night at a sauna party, as he was rambling on about Finnish business, he said something about how Finns showed no interest in Estonia because it was small and it was too risky, and how probably they would wait till the very end, because they always entered the market late in the cycle. It was one of those random conversations that you naturally forget about. I bought one of his CDs, played it once for about five minutes, and I forgot about him for the next fifteen years.

But in 2007, that casual conversation came back to me as a flashing red stop light when a Finnish private equity firm called me out of the blue one day to set up a meeting. After a lot of good coffee and several of the cinnamon buns the Finns are famous for, it turned out what they wanted was to buy one of my businesses and merge it with their Scandinavian business.

At the time, selling anything was the last thing on my mind. I was happy and pretty well off. I could pretty much come and go as I pleased. With an office that hummed along in my absence, I could take time off and I went on some killer holidays. My property development company was booming, and I had a rolodex of joint venture partners I could call on with deals that got bigger as we went along.

By then I was also enjoying hanging out in London a lot and finding my way around bespoke tailors and shirt makers. In my spare time, I was running around the City, lining up investors for a new Central and Eastern European property fund; in the process of purchasing a publicly-traded company in Helsinki with an Israeli partner; flying back and forth to Germany to look at German residential portfolios with a real estate private equity firm based in New York; and spending time at my ranch and home in Argentina which I had purchased.

But at that meeting, after some good Finnish coffee and a few cinnamon buns, that sauna conversation came flashing back and I had an epiphany, "aha!", a lightbulb moment.

And just like that, with no more than a hunch, and despite all that I was doing in a market that seemed like it would never go down, I made the decision to sell all my businesses. To be honest, I'd like to say I was super smart and had the foresight, but actually my exit was about as well planned as my entry. Thanks to Elvis, the rest, as they say, is history.

The lightbulb moment paid in spades. As luck would have it, just as the last business sold in 2008, the financial crisis hit one week later, and the global economy crashed as we all remember. I'd happily left the Kool-Aid bowl just in time. The music stopped, and I was out and suddenly I was extremely liquid. As everything nosedived over the coming two years, I was hailed as a market guru. Dumb luck timing. I call it my Forrest Gump moment. I still have the picture!

....

BACK IN 1987, I was a New York futures and equity options trader. I was young and prone to be pretty stupid at a time when most of my peers were trying to be responsible. I loved to party all night and then rocked up to the trading floor each morning, my head pounding and sometimes still massively hung over from a night out at Elaine's or the Surf Club.

Then one day, I woke to find myself out of a job.

No surprise to anyone maybe.

Big surprise for me.

I was suddenly almost broke, and I was totally embarrassed. From where I stood, things looked pretty bleak. At that moment, I couldn't have been further away from eating cinnamon buns in Helsinki with a bunch of private equity guys. But that is where my journey took me. All on its own. All I did was show up, step in loads of shit, learn from my mistakes, then get the job done every day. Easier said than done.

All the great things I was able to do and participate in were never planned out in some great master plan. I worked hard, tried new things, and kept moving; shit happened that I could have never dreamed up alone. In the end, all the "luck", and all my "stuff" came bit-by-bit and accumulated almost naturally. I was never really looking for any of it. Ever. I was like a passenger.

Actually, my dog probably could probably have taught me the same; stay away from big mean dogs, keep moving and hustle for every crumb, and just wait. Be patient.

Trust me, forget the "Ten Secrets to Success" or the stuff they try and sell you on social media. The real secret is you need to take a different path, work hard and let go of outcomes. For me, that meant starting in a market I knew nothing about and building from that. Kind of like selling tacos in Africa.

I had no connections, and I didn't even speak the language of the countries I did business in. I started with pocket change, wrote a few business plans for a grub-stake of some cash, and then built a portfolio of businesses worth more $200 million over 18 years.

And yes, if I want to start comparing, sure, there are loads of people who have made tons more money than me in a shorter period of time, but given where I started from, where I was in my head, and the obstacles I encountered along the way, I'm still pretty amazed it happened at all. And to be honest, I'm pretty proud of that.

Building that business took time. But when you are in the groove, and you know somehow that it's right, time flies by. Those 18 years went by in the blink of an eye. Ask any successful entrepreneur and I think they'll say the same. Time just flies.

You start down a path, course correct as you go, and don't give up. Also, just as a side bar; it's never about the money. It is always about just doing it and making it work every day. It's all about solving the next problem; it's a process, not an overnight transformation. It's always about solving the next problem.

Frankly, I know of no overnight successes.

During my problem-solving process, I was fortunate enough to meet and work with some great people who became like family. As a team, we created things. We achieved tangible results we could point to, and that's always a good thing.

Eventually, it made us all a lot of money—and we had fun doing it. But money was never the goal. We really never thought of what we were doing as work; we were always solving problems and trying stuff out and when it worked, we did more of that. It was better than having a hobby. We went in early and left late because we didn't want to stop having fun.

I personally think the key to happiness and even wealth is being able to find that place in life where you feel useful to others. The more useful you are, the happier you'll be. And when you are happy, things just seem to work out all by themselves. By the way, that kind of thinking comes after learning just what it feels like when you don't feel useful anymore. Maybe all we're ever trying to achieve in life is to be useful.

And when we're not useful we feel lost, get stuck and feel depressed. But if you are useful, you'll probably create a lot of value for lots of people, and end up with some great friends. It's hard work. It also helps having the wind at your back, like I did with markets booming. But, bottom line, the luck comes from just showing up every day, not from just wishing and making vision boards. And you can't show up every day unless you feel useful and are genuinely happy.

·······

REMEMBER THE STORY of Jack and the Beanstalk? Poor and destitute, Jack's mom asks him to go to market and sell the cow for money to buy food. Jack, young and impressionable, gets conned along the way, sells the cow, takes the money, and ends up buying some "magic beans". When he comes home, he is sent to his room for being so stupid, where he falls asleep and dreams of great riches in the sky at the end of a giant beanstalk.

Of course, we all know the movie; when he wakes up, they still had no food and no cows.

We all want to believe Jack's dream though. We all want things to happen right now. We all want those magic beans but sadly, there are none. Just look at all the big businesses selling dreams on today's social media. We're all so hungry to find happiness and to find the secret to success, that we spend hours reading book after book, and spend tons of money chasing ideas that others are more than happy to sell us. There's always another sucker.

The key is to find something, get good at it gradually, and be useful.

Think of it like a puzzle. At any given moment, you don't know exactly where all the pieces fit quite yet, but you will figure it out. Entrepreneurship is about figuring out the puzzle and with it comes the thrill (and pain) of exploration, and about finding what works and what doesn't. Maybe you need to be a bit stupid to know that it just might not work in order to keep trying.

I have no "magic beans" to sell you.

But . . . while I was writing the next eighteen chapters of this book, something else happened. Over time, my book title and its original purpose took on a different meaning for me. It happened one day after I met a complete stranger in a Chelsea café on Sloane Square in London. That meeting challenged me. It inspired me to set out on a several new adventures of my own again. Some that are working, some that are still in progress, some that have failed, and one path I know well and which I came back to; being useful.

·······

MOST PEOPLE THINK they need to get from A to Z in a straight line—as the crow flies. Yes, it's a bonus if you have a well thought out plan. But I've come to realise that life isn't quite so simple. Those well thought out plans will always change. Anyway, if it were that simple, life would be pretty boring. If I do this, I get this, and then that happens—job done! How boring is that really?

As a result, I never underestimate what life might have in store for me. In 1992, getting on that plane, I was still a kid deep down, I was only five years sober and without any money or any real skills that I could think of. At least that's what I saw—but the universe had other plans for me, as I would soon find out.

I believe that somehow successful people are driven by their circumstances, and then use those circumstances to stumble across opportunity. Without knowing it, my childhood wounds, my Wall Street excess and addictions, my recovery and finally my trip to Estonia were the connect-the-dot moments that provided the opportunities that would unfold. And by 2008, like dominoes, they had all fallen into place in one quantum moment.

From that plane trip in early1992, I had built seven companies; I had helped start a bank, a mortgage company, and developed the largest retail and commercial real estate company in the region. Without really knowing it at the time, I had become one of the largest property developers in Eastern Europe, building over three million square feet of commercial retail space alone.

I mean, how does that happen, really? My goal had been to go to graduate school and get a business degree—that was my A-to-Z plan, that was my magic beans, that was my Doris day narrative. I'd bought into that movie.

But I missed that goal by a mile. Thinking about it now, I realise it wasn't really ever my goal. It was one of those things we do because everyone else seems to be doing it, so it must be right. It was like a box I should tick off; but deep down, it wasn't me at all.

I decided to stay in Estonia and bypass business school, and ultimately I ended up in a far better place, achieving something far more special than I ever could have managed to plan on my own.

And over a period of eighteen years, I found myself. And as I did that, I was also able to pull together a team of colleagues who helped me night and day. Together we built a remarkable set of businesses. At our peak, we had some 650 employees on the ground, in a network that spanned five countries.

Yet no matter what the circumstances of each of our lives, I believe that there are certain things that make entrepreneurs different from the rest; I think it's some combination of mixed-up DNA that profiles all of us. We all have it. What makes us stand out and push harder than most people in my opinion, are our self-perceived weaknesses and our self-perceived fears. It's just a matter of recognising how these two demons have shaped us, and then build on those and the behaviours, take that energy and bring them out in a positive way.

For me to have gotten on the airplane with little more than a return ticket (which I never used), meant that I had to let go of a lot of stuff and move ahead into an uncertain future and put those demons in the past before moving on.

I had to let go of fear, and the ingrained beliefs and stories I had bought into and had been sold. I had to just let stuff happen. And at some point, the dots started to connect by themselves.

That means facing all those perceived weaknesses and saying "No" to them. What matters is being open to the reality that you will probably end up somewhere better than your original plan.

Don't get me wrong, going with that approach can be scary. Leaving the pack is scary. Letting go of long held beliefs is scary. Starting again is scary. And yes, there are loads of times when I'd like to be the guy who commutes to work each day; the guy who has a real job title, who takes vacations at the same time every year and gets a regular steady paycheque.

Sometimes that idea just seems so attractive.

It's predictable. It's safe. It pays the groceries.

But the reality is that it's an illusion. There really is no job security the way there used to be, and people come and go. Tech has changed the world, and the world has become smaller. People can be replaced easily. The job I used to have trading on the floor as a pit trader is history. Most people today don't even know what that is. Floors like the Chicago Board of Trade, the Options Exchange, the Chicago and New York Mercantile Exchanges are all gone. The American Stock Exchange is a big empty building behind Trinity Church in New York and next to Ground Zero. All done away with by tech and smarter computers. You blink nowadays and everything has changed.

And anyway, even if there was that job security, a lot of those people who have those entrepreneurial callings like I did, will feel trapped and unfulfilled like I did. Just look around closely; there are a lot of unhappy people these days, just clocking time. Clipping a paycheque and hoping they will have a job tomorrow. That's such a waste of life. Most of them will never take that leap of faith, no matter what.

·······

THE NOT SO FUNNY THING ABOUT THE FUTURE is it's the one thing you can't see, and not being able to see can be a terrifying dark moment.

I remember curling in up in absolute fear and pain, alone in my studio flat, wondering how I was going to manage all the obstacles I faced, and wondering what was going to happen next. It's easy to look back and want things to be the same but looking back all the time keeps you stuck. You need to look ahead into the darkness and just go for it. Yes, it is scary, but no one dies.

So you may as well take the shot.

To have something different happen in your life, you have to stop watching the same movie over and over again. Get out of your comfort zone and go in a totally new direction. Firmly believe that success is right around the corner. A successful entrepreneur I know always says, "Don't leave before the miracle happens". I have always believed in miracles. An entrepreneur must be first and foremost an optimist.

And if I can do it, anyone can. And I still keep making mistakes. In twenty-nine years, I probably have made every mistake you could make. And I will surely find more. But I've also found that success leaves footprints and so I look for those footprints every day. Do the things you don't like to do and feel uncomfortable. If you can face your fears, your shadows, and put the past behind you, a whole lot of new experiences and surprises happen.

Over the course of my career, I've had to fund businesses out of pocket that weren't working fast enough, step on suppliers' payments, stretch cash flow as far as possible and do a whole lot of super uncomfortable things.

In Eastern Europe, I've had guns pulled on me by mafia, and investors let me down at the very last minute. And all of this while keeping the lights on. But here's the thing; looking at it now, I wouldn't have wanted it any other way. All these uncomfortable things have made me who I am. And I'm confident that you could drop me anywhere in the world today with $400, and I could start again. It wouldn't be easy, it never is, but I know I could.

Okay, you're probably not going to pack up your family and move continents like I did. Fair enough. You don't have to leave your country or your neighborhood or change your existing business right away. But you need to look at what you're doing and expecting, and generally know where you want to go, then you need to get up, get moving, and have faith. After all, most peoples' beliefs are based on past experience—what you know. Faith is something different; it's the willingness to believe in what you don't know.

THINGS TO THINK ABOUT

1. Don't dismiss chance meetings; someday those people or conversations will trigger an "aha" moment.
2. There are no Magic Beans; success is a series of small steps taken every day that eventually lead to single quantum moments.
3. The journey is never straight; there is no A-to-Z path.
4. The future is created by what you do every day under given circumstances. Choose wisely.

Chapter 2

IMPRESSIONS

> *The alphabet is the first step to wisdom.*
> —Russian Proverb

IN THE EIGHTEEN YEARS from when I left New York for Eastern Europe, I lived out what I'd envisioned so many years before; I just didn't know that was what was happening as I was living it. Without my consciously knowing it, with each step I took I was acting through a script I'd written for myself years before, editing and writing new chapters as I went along.

Today, as I look at the press clippings, photos, and the magazine covers, I wonder, "Did that really happen? Was that really me?" I mean really, WTF!

But it did happen. All of it. It now seems long ago. Sitting in my office today while starting yet another new business many years later, I wonder. I ask myself those questions a lot.

It was a part of me, but only a part. It was a moment in time.

Rewind. As a kid growing up in Illinois outside of Chicago in the 1960s, I saw a lot of shopping centers popping up in cornfields. I was fascinated by those big structures and all the machinery that built them. Hunched over the back of my new Schwinn bike I witnessed first-hand the Chicago sprawl of suburbs growing and new homes being built everywhere I looked. I remember sitting on my bike on a hilltop overlooking Turner's cornfield down the road from our house on Hattendorf Street and watching Chicagoland's first indoor shopping mall being built. Somewhere in the back of my seven-year-old mind, I decided that's what I wanted to do. I wanted to build stuff. I wanted to create stuff, own it and point at it. It was a moment.

I forgot that moment for a long time.

But those impressions of building, of equipment, of piles of timber, mountains of dirt and of concrete, made a mark on my little seven-year-old brain, and became part of my psychological DNA, hidden for years.

·······

AS A TRADER ON WALL STREET I didn't build anything. There was none of that sense of awe I had watching those building sites. What I did everyday felt empty and meaningless. As a futures and options trader, I was trading time related values against someone else doing the same thing. At the close of trading everyday all that remained were my trading sheets and crumpled-up order sheets—just numbers. Some of those numbers represented a profitable trade and some losing trades. The more winners the better, of course. Some days I made money, some days I lost money. Fundamentally, the problem was the money I earned and lost meant really nothing to me. There was really no value to what I was doing. Deep down, I wanted to do something better with my life, I just had no clue what that was.

Back then, and I think it's true for a lot of people, one of the internal struggles I always grappled with in those days, was the idea that I had to know everything. Of course, knowing everything is an impossible task. To be honest, I guess that's why I thought I needed to go to business school. I really didn't feel good enough, and I suppose I thought business school would solve that problem. It would make me respectable and teach me everything I wanted to know. The crazy thing is that most of us lead our lives trying to live by a play book written by other people; our parents, our communities, our friends. We want to be like everyone else and be accepted. At least I did. But most often that play book is wrong.

You will never know everything and the more you know, the more you find out you don't know. Thinking otherwise is a time waster. You simply don't need to know how to do everything. And yes there will always be smarter people. But eventually, you will figure it out. And if you look around you, you'll find loads of people out there, all doing the same thing, some of them with pretty fancy degrees from equally impressive schools—they are the one's that read the play book. They may look and sound like the real deal, but frankly, they couldn't manage their way out of a paper bag if they tried. They will never make any sort of real impact on anything or anyone in the short time we have on this planet. All they ever really wanted was a job.

But you will also be happy to hear that the wheel has already been built. There is no reason for you to know how to build it. People have done loads of stuff you can read about and you can find instructional videos on YouTube these days that will teach you to do just about anything. Your job is to figure out the problem and find the answer. Just ask.

Ask, and along the way, you will find people that will help. There are plenty of people with the skill set you need if you don't have them. Think about it like this; if you wait to achieve the 10,000-Hour Rule (meaning you need 10,000 hours of experience to be an expert), you will wait a long time. Try breaking down 10,000 hours. The real secret, if there is one, is that you can hire people or ask for 10,000 hours' worth of experience in a day. Most people just don't think that way.

I built over three million square feet of commercial retail shopping center space, five hotels, countless restaurants and fast food chains, and the largest real estate company in Central and Eastern Europe and when I started, I knew absolutely nothing about real estate.

How did that happen?

By asking, and time. Finding problems to solve and solving them; and then asking loads of people to help me.

Most of the guys I went to school with were smarter than me. Universities are full of smart people. But that doesn't mean they have what it takes. You need a degree to be a doctor, a scientist, a physicist, a veterinarian, a dentist, a psychologist. You do not need a fancy business degree to be successful in business. You do need one, however, to get a job if that's what you want. Degrees and grades are measurable and put you into a category.

·······

WATCHING ALL THAT BUILDING back in the 1960s had inspired me. I didn't know it at the time, and it took me years to peel back the onion, figure it out and build the faith I needed to do something different. But even today, ask me about building shopping centers and I would probably give you pretty disappointing advice, or ask me about kitchen fit-out or procurement for hotels? I either know nothing about these things or I know very little compared to the experts, and that's just fine. Practically speaking, my team and project managers built those businesses; I was the guy with the idea, and the guy that was crazy enough to keep pulling it all together and moving it forward, finding new problems along the way.

So I was the idea guy.

Bottom line, I think what you need far more than technical smarts is unmatched faith and the doggone unstoppable determination to make it work and of course, a worthwhile idea.

You can't look down and you can't overthink this.

Think back. Think about stuff that happened in your childhood, and impressions that were made. Dig and try to unearth what excited you. And when you find that thing, put it out there 100 percent, and then be open to anything, because once on course, life just happens unexpectedly, like John Lennon said.

·······

SHORTLY AFTER ARRIVING IN ESTONIA, I met a young Russian on the town hall square. His name was Sergei. After a few days, Sergei asked me to help him write a business plan for a new retail shop he wanted to open. He was looking to raise money from one of the newer banks in town and needed a loan but didn't know how to write a business plan. I didn't profess to be a whiz at this, but I gave it a go and wrote it for him. It was pretty basic and in English. Amazingly, he got the loan. I think we were both pretty surprised, and then he asked me how much I wanted, and paid me $500 in cash.

The next week, his friend came and asked me to do the same thing and I wrote another business plan. And same thing; amazingly, he got a loan as well. But this time, when his friend asked me what he owed me, I asked for $1,000. Now, I might be from the cornfields of Illinois, but I'm not stupid. He paid me and that's how it all started. That's how the shoeboxes got full of cash that summer.

I was suddenly in business without really trying to be. I was just solving a problem for someone.

One thing led to another, and from that small start, I started helping others do the same in quick succession. By the end of the summer, I was writing some full-scale business plans for some of the larger local businesses and some foreign; an Austrian hotel company for example, and I even wrote a market review for the Minister of the Economy. By then I had hired a few smarter people who would just pull it all together for me. A year later and I would begin writing what would become my own business plan about starting a real estate company.

Why real estate? It sort-of just happened.

You need to understand I was in a country where I didn't speak the language, and that made whatever I wanted to do difficult. It was serious problem. But I could see that no one was paying too much attention to real estate or prices. At the time, the big wheeler-dealers were trying to privatise companies from the government. I couldn't do that without being able to speak the language. But to my advantage, none of them at the time were thinking about spending time on building a house or flat.

More importantly, I needed a flat.

So I built one. My first real estate deal was building myself a flat in a soviet-style apartment building next to the American Embassy. When it was finished, as luck would have it, the Embassy wanted it and rented it out before I even moved in, so I needed to build another flat. And that was the beginning. One flat at a time.

I still have that original business plan and it became the start of a plan that I religiously updated every year for many years. I gave me a way forward and a vision to follow.

Writing it all down, having a general vision, and articulating it for my small team was critical. That early stage business plan was a critical step to growing the largest real estate company in Central and Eastern Europe. It happened one step at a time; starting with writing Sergei's business plan, then flat by flat.

I was connecting the dots and I didn't even know it. From Schwinn bikes in Illinois, to Wall Street, years of recovery, to finding my way to Estonia. But once I knew what I really wanted to do, everything became easy and fell into place. Once I got that story down in my head, it was easy for me to share that story with others. Because I was excited, other people got excited and got on the bus.

THINGS TO THINK ABOUT

1. Understand that opportunities come from your unique circumstances in life. You can try all you want to force things, but only by connecting the dots do opportunities unfold. You may need to change some things about your life and take some scary steps.
2. Wait and be patient. Just show up and be open-minded. As you watch the people and businesses around you, you'll start to see opportunities and figure out what triggers your imagination.
3. When you find your vision let it sink in, see if it still excites you in a week or so. If it does, write it down into an exciting story.

4. Share that story and vision with others. As you hone both your vision and your storytelling skills, you'll inspire a team to gather around you and your vision. This team is vital to your success.

Chapter 3

BELIEVING

The secret to getting ahead is getting started.
—Mark Twain

WHAT I FOUND IN AA RECOVERY was that in order for me to cope and get through life's challenges I needed to believe in something greater than myself. I had to learn to surrender. When things get tough, trying to carry the world on your shoulders is heavy. Most shit I can't control anyway, so trying was an impossible and exhausting undertaking.

In my 1980s *Bonfire of the Vanities* days, my belief in God came from desperation, as my head was spinning and I found myself praying at the toilet bowl, promising I'd never drink again.

Of course, not everyone has that kind of biblical toilet bowl experience. But I'm sure some of you will know what I'm talking about. Of course, my prayers were never answered, and of course, I never kept my promise to God, either.

Today, thanks to that recovery program, I have a strong spiritual foundation and a belief in a Power Greater than myself. Call it a Universal Presence, God, or whatever, but I believe this spiritual foundational has been paramount to any of my success and has helped me immensely when things got pretty tough. At least, that's how I figure it today. Before I came to that understanding, I struggled to control everything with great effort and with even greater disappointment. Somewhere in my thinking, I thought I had to control everything and everyone. And it never worked as I'd planned.

As I pushed and pulled through my life, trying to control the world and force things to work my way, it only just seemed to get harder. I was constantly pushing up against people and circumstances that were beyond my control; and when life would throw me some additional curve balls just for kicks, my only defence was to blame everyone and everything and get upset. It was exhausting.

....

RECENTLY, I WAS TRYING TO CLOSE A DEAL that had already died ten times in two weeks. Each time we'd fixed the problem and thought we were done; we'd go through a series of premature "high fives" and celebrate. Now with the closing a day away, we were on our way to a weekend away with the team. As we were looking at the flight departure board, moaning about the two-hour delay the phone rang. It was our lawyer.

Our deal was dead again. Everyone freaked out. The other side's lawyers and ours were stuck on a point and in a professional gridlock. Worse still, we were getting emails from our bankers asking what the F was going on, and they wanted to pull their funding line immediately. They wanted and were waiting for a response.

My colleague wanted to text and phone the bankers right back. He had no idea what he was going to say, he just felt he needed to make a series of phone calls. He paced up and down and kept saying, "We need to call them. We need to respond now". But I knew we didn't have all the info. I urged him to just wait. He had his finger on the phone.

We used the two hour delay to figure out what had happened, then when we were ready; we organised a call between lawyers and invited the bank on the phone. It was a long two hours of waiting and thinking, but it was a ten-minute call. We solved the problem.

Had we reacted in knee-jerk fashion, trying desperately to control things, making that call, we would have looked like total idiots.

In recovery, I learned to take small leaps of faith into the unknown and let go of the results. That kind of faith allowed me to let go of trying to have everything perfect and control every outcome – right now. When I do that, things seem to fit together easier.

·······

DEALING WITH EVERYDAY life situations gracefully isn't at all easy and having to accept things as they are can be equally difficult. Trust me, even today, after some 33 years of thinking this way, some days can seem downright impossible to get through. But it's in those tough moments that you learn. You learn that when you are getting so close to a goal that you can see and feel it, suddenly those curve balls come at you hard and fast, that's when the Universe is asking you the BIG questions; how much do you really want this, and, are you ready for it?

The idea of wanting to be in control of everything can be pretty overwhelming, to say the least. Sometimes, you just need to pause, let go and wait.

In those difficult situations, the only thing that gets me out of bed each morning, without wanting to throw myself under a bus, is the total trust that I am doing the right thing and that somehow, I will be taken care of. Of course, letting go does not mean being complacent. It just means being able to do stuff without expectation. Like my dog.

....

YEARS LATER, after my home-run of successes and retiring at 48, I learned this lesson again. I took the well-deserved opportunity to blow through loads of cash on a lot of lifestyle stuff and ego enhancing hobbies and toys. Super fun stuff.

Rightly so, I had felt I had earned the privilege of acquiring what I wanted, whenever I wanted. It never occurred to me that I was blowing through cash so fast, isolating and digging myself into a big black hole that would be terribly difficult to dig out of. What made it worse, was after those successes, I started to believe all the press clippings. And it all became about me.

I'd forgotten the truths of usefulness, hard work, persistence and teamwork, letting go and instead I just ran away with my money. I'd forgotten about the people who had supported me, and I slowly I started losing my feeling of usefulness to the world. And in the process, I'd lost the most valuable asset I'd actually been given; my happiness.

How?

By gradually forgetting.

In life, you really don't want to relearn hard lessons. At least for me, after running like a machine for 18 years and turning it off for ten years, starting it back up again was like pushing a boulder up a mountain. When you stop, you lose momentum. It's even harder the second time.

I was back to trying to control outcomes; blaming and building up huge resentments; in other words, feeling rather alone and useless—much like my last days of binging on addiction and losing my job on Wall Street. It was a terrible feeling. So back to basics I went, piecing together the puzzle I'd broken apart and searching for the missing pieces. On top of the seemingly insurmountable odds and trying to figure it all out again, it's also a truly humbling experience.

Gradually, I had to find faith again and get going. It took three painful years to get that boulder to even budge. I kept wanting to look back and think that things hadn't changed. But they had. I'd also changed, and I wasn't 30 years old anymore. Today, it is faith that gets me out of bed each day again and keeps me going when others would have simply given up.

·······

BELIEVE IN SOMETHING—call it God, a group of colleagues, your family, school, or even your business idea. But you need something solid that gets you moving when the shit hits the fan. You can't just sit there and feel sorry for yourself or look backwards. That's done with. That was yesterday's news. You need to get up and get going and enter that dark place called tomorrow by doing things today in faith and with determination. And who knows where this ends up finally, but you strap in and get ready for the journey. And I found that you need to forget what other people think.

The status quo is the place most people want to live. But what I've found is nothing stands still, and things don't wait.

Things change, people change, circumstances change. Our natural tendency is to revert to behaviours and ways of doing things that are safe and which seem secure, and may have worked once before, but at the same time that kind of thinking and response keeps you stuck. And being stuck is a terrible place to be.

In business, as in life, things change, sands shift, tick-tock the clock keeps moving, and sometimes things go wrong. But if you believe that your goal is right around the corner, you can stampede through the bandits of your mind. Blind faith moves you away from "it can't be done". It gives you that craziness that keeps you going. Faith protects you from naysayers and well-meaning friends who don't want you to change and would like you to safely stay exactly where you are.

·······

IN 1992, I HAD NO IDEA what my plans were going to be; I didn't know how things would work out. The only thing I knew for certain was that they would work out, somehow.

I landed in a dingy smoke-filled airport in Tallinn Estonia, surrounded by abandoned Soviet military vehicles, and headed into a city where I didn't know anyone. I had $400 to last me three weeks. But there was something exciting about not knowing anyone in a new environment. I was alone, and yet I knew I was in the right place.

I learned that you only have to show up, and shit happens. But how many people would get on an airplane with $400 and run off to an unknown country to start again? Not many, I assure you.

If you don't believe in yourself—I mean, believe enough

to bet the ranch and sacrifice precious time that can never be recaptured—don't do it. You need to believe. And when you believe, people help. People follow people who believe. You need people, and a business cannot be built without them, so you need to have that blind faith in what you are doing so you can share it. Without that kind of faith, no one is going to help you on your journey.

Faith is contagious.

Decide what you want and believe you can have it. Even if it seems out of reach at the moment. Practice being grateful for what you've been given, no matter how small that is, and move in the direction you want to go.

Life is a decision, and no one can make that decision but you. Ask yourself if you are willing to build that kind of faith. Do you believe? Do you have enough faith to take a different path and get on with it? My wife likes to say you can't read the next chapter if you keep re-reading the last one. Faith gives me the courage to turn the page.

THINGS TO THINK ABOUT

1. Find something bigger than yourself to believe in. You can't control everything, so you need to trust in something beyond yourself.
2. You can only control how you respond to things. That's it. Trust me on this one.
3. Believe in yourself and whatever you choose to do. Whatever that is, it is the thing you are meant to do. If you determine you were meant to do something, any obstacle is just an inconvenient annoyance you can overcome.

4. Show up and take that first leap forward. Sure, it's scary to step outside your comfort zone, to try to do what no one else is doing.
5. Turn the next page in life and don't look back. Faith is contagious. Build your business with people who are inspired by your leadership and your blind faith in what you are doing.

Chapter 4

SURRENDER TO WIN

> *Regardless of how you begin your careers, it is important to realize that your life will not necessarily move in a straight line.*
> —Steven A. Schwarzman, CEO Blackstone

BUILDING ANYTHING WORTHWHILE takes time and a commitment to let go of the end result. It takes the ability to listen to that small voice inside you, and not to other's opinions or agendas. It's about just doing the next thing every day, and not being too concerned with how much money you can make.

But you need to surrender to the idea there is a load of stuff you simply can't control and to be able to know the difference between what you can and can't. After a lot of years, I think the only thing any of us can control is how we respond or react to any given situation.

Funny thing about listening to your intuition and starting down a new path is that there will be huge internal resistance, and most of your closest friends and family will discourage you. People like the status quo and when one day you decide to be different, or to do something different it forces them to examine themselves. They won't like the changes. It's scary for them, too.

It's easy to be swayed by the opinions of other people. Go ahead and listen of course, but don't let their well-meaning

intentions determine your future. Chances are, they won't want
you to change. Just remember that.

So, go with your intuition. Listen to what's inside you.

·······

ONCE I DECIDED TO FINALLY STAY in Estonia and reboot
my life, all kinds of doors opened up for me. I met people, and
things happened; it was like I was just along for the ride. But
first, I had to make that choice. On my own, by myself. I had to
surrender to whatever outcome there would be.

When I was in my 12 Step Program there was this guy
in Westport, Connecticut at the Monday night men's meeting who used to end each meeting with a loud shout and say,
"Surrender to Win."

George was a crazy kind of guy; he even looked a bit
crazy with wild hair, a walking cane and eyes that bulged out,
probably someone you'd be intimidated by if you saw him
in any other social environment. But he had been sober for
something like 30 years so there was a lot of wisdom in there
somewhere. That shout, "Surrender to Win" always stayed with
me. I've thought about that statement over the years, and over
time I came to realise that it's a super powerful concept and has
helped me countless times.

When you surrender, you let go of the outcome. You let go
of control. You surf the wave. You make a commitment and then
there's only one thing to do after that; show up every day and
solve problem after problem, and ride the wave as it comes.

William Hutchison Murray, a famous Scottish mountain-
eer, wrote a book called *The Scottish Himalayan Expedition*
in 1951. The book explains in the beginning the start of an

incredible adventure and a faithful commitment to a dangerous journey:

"We had put down our passage money—booked a sailing
to Bombay . . . until one is committed, there is hesitancy, the
chance to draw back, always ineffectiveness. . .. Whatever you
can do or dream you can, begin it. Boldness has genius, power
and magic in it!"[i]

When I finally determine what I really want, a weight falls
off my shoulders. As any entrepreneur will tell you, you must
first make that decision, not look back and keep at it. Steve
Jobs, the founder of Apple, said something like, we are all going
to die anyway so really there is nothing to lose. Once that commitment to surrender is made, I find it much easier to get on
with whatever I'm meant to do.

·······

THERE'S THIS MASSIVE SWIMMING POOL I used to go
to in the summer at a private club in Argentina. The water was
always ice-cold. You had to climb up stairs to get to a platform
topped by a diving board.

I'd watch young teenage kids doing all kinds of back flips
and somersaults. It looked terrifying. How did they do that?
Just run up there and flip backwards? Not on my life. I couldn't
fathom the thought.

One day, I was with my son. He was watching those kids
and I could tell he wanted to give it a go. He was four or five.
He closely studied the other kids, and then he looked at me. I
knew it was my turn.

I took his hand, and we climbed up the stairs to the

i   Murray, William Hutchison. *The Scottish Himalayan Expedition.* 1951. Pg 7 platform. I knew I couldn't ask him to do something I couldn't do. I was afraid of diving boards and heights. As I looked down, my legs froze.

When I saw him looking at me, I made a decision right there not to let my fear dictate what I could do. I told him to watch; I explained to him I wasn't very good but that I would try anyway. I surrendered the outcome. And I did it. It was fine. I didn't kill myself. He happily jumped in after me. Once I made a commitment and surrendered, my son gladly followed. It works that way. So don't play small, choose instead to play big. Surrender and take the leap.

Of course, the scary part of committing to anything is thinking about it over and over again. That's where surrender comes in. Surrender does not mean you stop trying. Not at all. The paradox is that surrender is the switch that you can flip on to keep going, despite everything going wrong.

Stop thinking and take the plunge. Don't get me wrong—this is not easy, and I still look for all kinds of excuses to avoid decisions.

Today, at least I'm more capable of recognising my procrastination, and I force myself to move forward. I've learned that nothing can stop me but my own thinking. As Nike says, "Just do it." Ask yourself, what is one thing you have been procrastinating about because you're afraid to face it or fearful of making a major mistake? Do you think you are able to do that one thing? Surrender to win and just let go of control.

If you had to walk around the world, you could do it. How do you know? You know because once you take that first step, it's one step at a time, and eventually you'll arrive. You just need to take that first step and keep going, and each step becomes easier and easier.

THINGS TO THINK ABOUT

1. Don't let other people decide your future. Make your own decision. By listening to others, you give away your ability to act. Go with the small inner voice. Decide if this is what you want to do.

2. Make a commitment and surrender to that decision and the outcome. Entrepreneurs must make decisions and not look back; this frees you to move forward.

3. Surrender to win. Have faith in whatever it is you decide and let go of the results.

4. Take the first step. Stop thinking and take the plunge. Remember, a series of single steps is all it takes to eventually arrive at your goal. That first step can be hard, but they all get easier after that.

5. Trust in the miracle. Once you've made your decision, committed to it, and taken the first step, you'll be amazed at how many doors open up for you. You'll never know until you try.

Chapter 5

REBOOT

Stay hungry, stay foolish.
—Steve Jobs

A **COUPLE OF YEARS AGO,** I got a message on LinkedIn from a young Nigerian living in London. He had started a business in England, using some of his native African products to create a cool new soft drink, and had read about me somewhere and wanted to connect and ask for some advice. His name was Tula.

I accepted his invitation and thought nothing more about it. A few days later, I got an email message asking if I'd meet with him. He explained how he had decided to start this business and wanted to know if I could help. Normally, I don't meet total strangers in cafés, but something about his approach reminded me of me; I wanted to learn more about this guy, so I met with him.

We met in London, in a café on Sloane Square. The same café where I used to take my son and wife to breakfast on the school run in the morning. It was close to my apartment and I could walk over easily. Today, it's one of my favourite short business meeting places—it does cook the best eggs. The interesting thing about the meeting was that it actually gave me the title for this book.

Tula has quit his job and started this drinks company and

now he was unsure he had done the right thing. What was going through his mind was all the typical BS we all think about over and over again when we start something new; afraid it won't work, afraid you are not ready, afraid you don't have all the information . . . you don't have all the answers and need more time.

I think that's how most of us operate. We all hate the unknown and would rather not take any chances and let things carry on as they are. Why risk it, right? Better to just talk about it.

The upside of course, is that since most people think that way, anyone who thinks differently and just tries begins with a distinct advantage. And the Bigger the challenge or goal, the less competition there will be. If you can get your head around that, you'll be far down the road before anyone else gives it a go.

·······

IN THE BOOK *A More Beautiful Question*, by Warren Berger, he talks about an interesting experiment measuring a group of kindergarten children's success with a problem-solving exercise against a group of Harvard MBA students.

The two groups were divided and given spaghetti, string, tape, and a marshmallow and told to assemble the tallest structure they could in fifteen minutes. The outcome is probably no surprise.

The Harvard students spent too much time arguing about the project and who would be in charge of what. Meanwhile, the children jumped right in and worked in what seemed like chaos, adapting quickly to small successes and failures as the tower kept falling down. The kids won, of course.

As Berger describes, "the point of the marshmallow

experiment was not to humble MBA students (if anything, that was a side benefit), but rather to better understand how to make progress when tasked with a difficult challenge in uncertain conditions."[ii] What we learn from this is the power of just cracking on and trying things quickly to see what works and what doesn't.

In my first few months in Estonia, after I had saved enough money from writing business plans, I started to hire people and moved into my first office. At first, there was only my assistant and me. It wasn't much, and we were no super hero team by any stretch of the imagination.

Soon after, I had three people on my team. We still had no idea what we were doing, and everyone in the market ignored us. We borrowed things we needed, and we asked for favours.

When you're starting out, it's easy to make mistakes; and if you start small, those mistakes don't cost much. In those early days, it's easy to shut down the whole thing if it doesn't work and start again or change tracks. Once your model is proven and working, then of course a full court press, but in the beginning, start small and stay away from the big stuff; the mean angry dogs! The key is to start. Just start, hustle, and don't worry if you don't have all the answers. Learn as you are building. If you're wrong, you can make adjustments and get the model right.

Most people want to start Big.

They want, and they expect the end result right now!

We are told to think Big, be Big, play Big.

That's great, and you move towards that for sure, but in the beginning, take baby steps. Big comes in time.

---

ii   Berger, Warren. *A More Beautiful Question: The Power of Inquiry to Spark Breakthrough Ideas.* 2014 Bloomsbury: New York. 121.

When you start Big you get overwhelmed with Big things, things you know nothing about. Starting Big also takes money. And the mistakes are Bigger too.

Starting small means that you are flexible, and there is little to lose. You can always start over again like the kids did with their spaghetti and marshmallow structure. Don't overthink things.

·······

AS I SAT WITH TULA THAT DAY at the café, I listened to his business idea. He was thinking big, and he was scaring the shit out of himself. The thought of having quit his job and the money he needed to raise was a lot to take on. He was building a factory in his head. He'd never built a factory in his head before and was pretty confused.

After my business plan writing days, I started to renovate apartments and sell them. That was our business in the beginning.

At any given moment, I could have folded the tent and moved on. We built one unit at a time, then two and then a few more. It was step-by-step.

Eventually, we grew. It was organic. We had to add on operations: bookkeepers, accountants, and a marketing and sales staff. Fast forward, by 2006, we were a team of 650 employees in 35 offices across Central and Eastern Europe. Like those kids in the spaghetti experiment, we just cracked on, and every time we hit a roadblock, we went another way. But we kept on and we grew and shit happened out of the blue that we couldn't make up if we tried.

It's tempting to want to have everything perfect before you

launch into something new. It's also a great excuse to never get started. Thinking too big can overwhelm you. You can think big once you know what you're doing. But overthinking saves us from trying and failing. It protects our sensitive egos. Fear of failure, embarrassment, ridicule, or being lost scares most of us.

Didn't we grow up believing we had to do things correctly?

In school, our teachers graded our exams by marking whether we'd answered the questions correctly or not. We are drilled not to make mistakes. Our mindsets are focused on knowing all the answers. At least that was the way I used to think. Tula was thinking that, too.

The bottom line is that we are afraid to make mistakes, so we don't push the boundaries and try.

It always starts with a step. A small step.

One deal. One step.

Two deals, then three.

Before you know it you will have more deals and a bigger business and more opportunities that you probably never even thought about.

Only a step. Just like my first dive off the diving board, your venture doesn't need to be perfect at the start. That will come with time.

·······

LIKE TULA, maybe you have a business idea or are thinking of quitting your job and setting out on your own. Good idea! But, you are hesitant and of course you are; you are afraid it won't work. That's only natural. I mean, who wants the embarrassment of failing?

Maybe you think you are not ready. You don't have all the

information. You don't have the pedigree or skill set. You don't have all the answers and need more time. Maybe taking some courses or going back to school is the answer. So you think some more. You talk to even more people. You end up getting even more confused.

Think back to Warren Berger's experiment with the spaghetti.

We need to be more open and trusting in the process; like kids really. You're going to make mistakes, that's a fact. Hopefully, a lot of mistakes if you're lucky. Then learn as you build. Start small, don't try to build big in the beginning. Gain confidence, gain skills and learn. And by the way, forget about the competition. It's out there sure as day, anyway.

No matter what you are thinking of doing or changing, there will be competition. Unless of course, you happen to stumble onto something that's going to change the world (and there are those people of course—many—who do) chances are someone is already doing what you are about to do. That is a good thing. You can learn from them and try and make it better or different. Thing is, you need to make it your own. But you need to choose, and you need to make that commitment. Taking a decision and making a commitment are two powerful forces that open doors.

And most people don't do either.

THINGS TO THINK ABOUT

1. Look at the opportunities available in your circum-stances, understand what you are passionate about, and create a vision for your business and your future. Then commit to that decision.

2. Pick one thing and do that. It always starts with a small step. That's it. Only a step.

3. Start now and don't hesitate. Put fear aside. Most people are afraid of being wrong. So they don't act. Just starting gives you a distinct advantage.

4. Just leap. There is power in just cracking on and trying things to see what works and what doesn't.

5. If it doesn't work or you make a mistake, try something new. Learn as you build. When you're wrong, make adjustments until you get the model right.

Chapter 6

THE NARRATIVE

> *You've got to sell your vision over and over again.*
> —Steven A. Schwarzan, CEO Blackstone

WELL, MY MEETING with the young Nigerian left me intrigued, and I started researching Africa and his product idea. I jotted down some ideas and made lists of things to check out. My new friend was struggling though, and he had done just about everything wrong he could possibly do. Especially on the financial side of things. But I liked his brand, and I liked his idea. It was cool.

I decided to look into it more closely. I walked down to Ryman's office and stationary store on King's Road in Chelsea and purchased a spiral notebook to work on this project.

Years earlier, when I was writing admissions essays for the top business schools I wanted to go to, a lot of it was about what I wanted to do with my future.

What I didn't realise at the time, was that all the things I was writing about would eventually come true. I learned that actually taking all those ideas and putting them down on paper makes you really think things through, and sometimes what seemed like a good idea at the time doesn't seem like such a good idea when you really try to explain it on paper.

That's why I'm always writing stuff down.

Writing is a powerful tool and a key skill for anyone who

wants to build anything or do anything. The narrative you end up with becomes your story. And at the end of the day, that's what people invest in. Stories. Stories that make sense and capture people's imaginations. Take Nike. Nike is and always has been simply a sporting shoe. But Nike doesn't sell shoes, they sell an idea of what those shoes represent. That's what people buy into.

Entrepreneurs become great by inspiring their investors, their customers and their team with a story, a vision. That excitement is contagious; you attract good people who will follow, and all kinds of good things happen.

I don't think Tula ever took the time to really sketch it all out.

It's hard to write. Try it. Even writing a memo is hard. Most people just give up. All those ideas get jumbled up. You end up with writers' block. Idea block.

That great idea might not be easy to articulate. And it also may feel a bit silly writing out stuff in grandiose ways, cutting out pictures and mapping things out that don't exist yet. It all may feel a bit fantastic. But I assure you, it works. And there is history from the beginning of time that proves this.

If writing ideas down is a powerful tool, then constructing those ideas into real story-like narratives may be the most powerful tool of all. Best to write them and not talk too much about them initially because it will change many times before you get it right.

········

WRITING IS ACTION, and it takes the idea from your mind to paper, then to an action plan to follow. It sounds easy but next time you have an amazing idea go ahead and try writing it down. You will find that suddenly you might end up with only a short paragraph, much of which may make no sense in the beginning. Writing forces you to dissect. Most people don't do it properly, or they simply give up or don't do it at all.

Also, the worst thing you can do is have someone else write it up for you. It's just not the same. That writing needs to come from you because it's emotional, it's your thing, not someone else's. It's inner voice trying to come out and it belongs only to you. No one has that idea except for you, at least initially.

And when you write, all kinds of things happen. New ideas emerge. Problems surface, opportunities appear out of nowhere. When you finally get it all down, your brain will have gone through an amazing process and will keep on trying to solve for things even when you're not thinking about it. Your plan will remain in your subconscious, and while you're not looking, it will find a way to manifest itself. Jung called this "synchronicity";—when events coincide with what you have mapped out in your mind.

Constructing those ideas on paper invites God or the Universe to help. When you write, you will be one of the few people who actually take that critical step, and this is a key advantage.

．．．．．．．

MOST PEOPLE JUST TALK ABOUT THINGS. You know the type. They dream. Bouncing around crazy ideas one week from the next. It's pretty easy to do. I do it. Everyone does.

But the vast majority sit behind a bar or at a dinner party and just talk; they may eloquently share what they are going to do. Ever notice the people who actually get a lot of stuff done and play big don't really talk that much about their projects to many people?

Thing is, very few of those talkers take the time to sit down, figure it all out pen in hand, and sketch it out. So, if you can write down your plan, figure it out and create a story; simplify and streamline what's in your head and turn it into a real live action plan, you are more than halfway there. Then you just need to crack on.

Imagine you are building a house or a building. You need a well thought-out plan. You get an architect. Every architect needs to create a plan for the builder. Every builder has a plan. You can't construct a building without one. Everyone knows this, so why is it that so few people ever draft out a plan for their business or their life?

Early on, I wrote business plans for people. That entire process and exercise I was doing for other people taught me some big lessons. Then I wrote one for myself and my business later on. It was pretty basic. But it was a start. I kept making it bigger as I went along.

Your plan will grow and evolve once you start. Never stop creating that plan. It will grow as you grow and change as your business changes.

·······

TULA HAD NO PLAN. He had a half-baked idea. He had a pretty cool logo and a web page which he'd spent loads of money on, and a pretty big social media following. He had no sensible production plan, and no distribution whatsoever and certainly no budgets, cash flows or forecasts which would have told him how much money was being sucked into non-essential parts of his start-up. He was just feeding his ego with media "likes".

Like most successful businesses, my business started as something I did on the side. One unit at a time. Then, two then three and on we went, creating and building as we went.

In 1993, I was helping a friend in Estonia build up his credit department at a bank. At the same time, I needed a decent place to live, so I decided to take the money I'd earned writing business plans and build myself a cracking bachelor pad.

But instead of moving in, I realised I could make a lot of money renting it out. So I did that instead. Of course, then I needed to build another one. So I did that, too. Just like that, I started renovating apartments one-by-one and renting them out to embassy personnel in Tallinn. Maybe it wasn't part of my original plan, but it shows what can happen when you start with a plan and build on it as you go.

A year later, when I left the bank, I'd flipped about five apartments. To do that, I was using people at different real estate agencies to find inventory for me, and then sell those flats. Eventually, I asked a few if they wanted to work with me full time. That was the start of our retail agency business. Start and adjust as you go. I never intended to build and rent out flats.

It's a well-known fact that a pilot flying a plane is almost always off course once he starts. There are so many variables to flying that a plane spends 95% of its flight off its charted course. The weather, the wind, the rotation of the earth, and a variety of other factors shift an airplane off its intended flight plan. So, like a pilot who reevaluates their position and makes corrections to ultimately land exactly on target, you need to do the same. Why don't we do that with our lives?

Like that pilot, you need a plan and you will need to course-correct.

When you write something down, it gets clarified in your head. By writing, you create a powerful tool to make your goals come true. But like anything else, you will need to stay flexible and constantly revise as circumstances change.

THINGS TO THINK ABOUT

1. Dare to have dreams. Don't be afraid to have a Big goal, but start small.
2. Sketch out a draft version of your goals. Writing and storytelling are powerful tools and for anyone who wants to build a company.
3. Share your plan with other people to build the right team of employees, investors, and consultants.
4. Course-correct. Be flexible. and keep re-writing. Unexpected circumstances will require you to constantly revise as circumstances change.

Chapter 7

HELP IS FOR THE ASKING

> *Success is what happens to you when and if you survive all your mistakes.*
> —Mastin Kipp

IT TOOK ME YEARS to figure out it was okay to not have all the answers. Fear of embarrassment, my own lack of self-esteem as a kid, thinking maybe others were smarter or better than me made holding my hand up and asking questions only to be laughed at a daunting prospect. As kids we grow up being tested, graded and compared. I guess for some that works, but I think in general it doesn't. At school, we have been taught to think there is a right way and a wrong way to do things. Clearly, no one wants to be wrong.

We don't want to appear stupid, so we don't ask for help.

Now, years later, and a whole lot wiser I hope, I ask for help all the time. There is not a thing wrong with not knowing something. And don't be fooled by all the jargon out there. It only exists to make others feel stupid. Trust me, it's easy to learn the vocabulary. You'll find a lot of people hide behind that vocabulary to appear smart. Don't let that fool you.

Ask for help. It's the single most important thing you can learn to do in life. In fact, most people love helping others, especially those who are more successful. Go ahead and ask for directions; don't keep driving around the block looking for the gas station like your Dad did. It will drive everyone around you nuts. And it will drive you nuts as well.

....

MY NEW NIGERIAN FRIEND TULA needed help and he knew it. I was impressed he'd reached out and asked. That was smart. A complete stranger reaching out to another complete stranger. That's so cool. I could have easily said no, but when someone sincerely asks, it's hard to say no.

I could relate to what he was going through at the time and wanted to be helpful, so I met with him a few more times, tried to guide him to the right professionals I thought he should meet with.

In our meetings, I discovered was that he had surrounded himself with self-seekers; people who wanted to take advantage of him. With the little money he'd raised and his inexperience, he'd spent way too much on marketing and social media, launch parties and PR.

No real budget, no forecasts, and now, before even really starting he was in debt, unable to pay his suppliers. A lot of these people, as well as his investors (who he'd stopped speaking to) were chasing him. They wanted to be paid, and they wanted to know what was going on.

In desperation, and as a last resort, he had contacted me looking for a bailout. He wanted me to lend him money.

What he really needed was some sensible advice. The last thing he needed was a handout. That was the worst thing I or anyone else could have done for him. I would help Tula, but not by giving him a loan for his business.

·······

BACK IN THE DAY, I also needed help when I first started Ober-Haus, my real estate company. I asked a lot of questions, and I hired a lot of people who were all smarter than I was.

I might have been the clever guy with the idea, but I knew very little about the market and how things worked. So, to survive, I had to find out. Fortunately for me I was using my money at that point, and when you do that instead of raising money, you're automatically more frugal.

In the beginning, I found most people were happy to help me and give me advice. I spoke with a lot of professionals, and even though sometimes my inexperience made me feel a bit on the back foot, I found that not always knowing was a blessing in disguise; you tend to learn a lot more.

Not knowing allows also you to make shit up as you go along and try it out because you don't know any better, and it also forces you to rely on others; also a good thing.

Not knowing something means you have to ask a lot of questions. It means you start at the beginning. That's a good thing too. Not knowing forces you to dissect and access the problem. You don't need to have the answers to get started, you just need the questions. At some point, you go out and find people who know the answers, and you hire them and get them to work for you.

Because I worked in countries where I didn't speak the language, I was at a clear disadvantage every moment of the day. That forced me to hire people to do things and to delegate a lot of stuff. Most first-time entrepreneurs like to do everything themselves; they tend to be slightly controlling. But to be successful, you need to have others help you do things. You cover a lot more ground that way, and you don't need to be an expert in every facet of the business.

Find and hire smart people; "stars"—people smarter than you. If you start or stay alone, you get killed. But if you surround yourself with great people, at least you prolong death for a long time. And hopefully, if it does come in one way or another, your venture will have become super successful and you will too.

You need to delegate so you can work on growing the business—others will manage the business, and then others will do the day-to-day work.

Out of necessity, I learned to ask people to help me, and that allowed me the freedom to grow my vision and do many more things I was good at—like creating new stuff to work on.

·······

WHEN I STARTED HELPING MY FRIEND at the bank build his credit department, I knew nothing about banking. I asked for help. I hooked up with some accountants from PWC who were doing a countrywide bank assessment and audit for the government and they gave me the PWC credit handbook. Yes, it does exist. One page at a time, chapter by chapter, we put in place the systems we needed, and we build a large credit department from scratch. None of us had done anything like this before, but we never thought it wasn't going to work. Looking back, it was unheard of; starting a bank with a book!

Same thing when I started building apartments. I had never built anything before, so I hired professionals; architects, builders who had the expertise, and I hired good estate agents.

I learned that to be a real estate developer, it wasn't so much about knowing the technicalities, it as about pulling together the deal and the people.

My first flat was amazing . . . except we forgot to tell them we wanted lights! Yes, lights. Back then, things we so basic in these post-soviet countries you had to spell it all out or it wouldn't get done. So, the contractors delivered me a fully finished flat without lights.

When I started my retail real estate agency business, I knew nothing about real estate services, so I hired people from other agencies. I knew what I wanted and what it should all look like and what it should represent; I just didn't know how to do those things. So, I asked.

As an entrepreneur, there is narrative you need to construct first and then share in order to get buy-in and inspire people. There are the big goals and then there's all the stuff you actually need to do. I was and still am, pretty good at the first, but I'm rubbish at the details. So, I go find people who can help execute the details. My job has always been knowing what the questions are; other people's jobs are providing the answers to help me make decisions.

I think it's also a pretty good idea to hang with other entrepreneurs. Those who have been there before. Not all the time, because you can get lost in too many ideas, but sometimes; because otherwise who do you talk to about things that aren't working or all the concerns you might have?

You can't really confide your fears to your employees— that only backfires. You really don't want your team to know you are unsure or be concerned that you are freaking out. So, you need a group, or at least several individuals, you can talk to on a regular basis who have no direct interest in the business.

That can mean developing a good relationship with a lawyer or a corporate finance guy, if you're working with one. If you're lucky, you will stumble upon people who have been successful and may be retired and looking to pass on knowledge. An Advisory Board is always good to have.

If you have investors, they are also a good sounding board to bounce ideas off of. Naturally, they want you to succeed, so they tend to make themselves available for the important discussions. A lot of entrepreneurs will be too embarrassed to reach out when things go wrong. But that's exactly when you need to reach out. No one likes surprises.

Beyond that, I suggest getting involved with forums of like-minded people. Today, the internet is full of chat groups and forums that discuss specific topics. Some are free and some cost. But these are professional groups of business owners and entrepreneurs that all have the same issues you do, and that provides both a vital source of information. I know some people who have been going to the same groups for years, and they find it a huge help in overcoming business obstacles, and even personal issues, that they face as an entrepreneur.

THINGS TO THINK ABOUT

1. Pinpoint what you need to know. There will be many things you need to know that you don't. This is not a problem. You can't do everything yourself, and you can't be the best at everything. You need outside help.
2. Just Ask.
3. Don't ask for handouts when what you want is information. Your job is knowing what questions to ask and finding people who know the answers.

4. Hire professionals who know what you need to know. Most first-time entrepreneurs like to do everything themselves, but to be successful, you need to have others do things for you. You need to delegate.
5. Join a forum of like-minded business people or a master-mind group. Use this support system to gain and share knowledge and encouragement with other professionals who are walking the same path.

Chapter 8

GREAT TEAMS BUILD
BUSINESSES

Teamwork begins by building trust. And the only way to do that is to overcome our need for invulnerability.
—Patrick Lencioni

MY **WIFE LIKES TO REMIND ME,** "astronauts don't fly to the moon alone." She reminds me a lot because I need to hear it. And it's a good thing to remember, especially once you've hit pay dirt. I know that I should probably listen to her more. Because you can't ever forget that things get done with other people.

I need a good ground team. You cannot mentally know and physically do everything by yourself, even though sometimes I like to think I can do it all by myself. Think of it this way; you'll move a lot faster if you work as a team and let people get on with what they are good at. That's really the secret; build a culture and environment where everyone participates and is rewarded. And multiply effort.

You'd be surprised that the great people you will hire are less concerned with how much money you pay them, and more motivated by the reason; the story, the ethos, and the why of the business. Good people want to be part of something special, something new. New ventures, new adventures are far more appealing than money. I think it's written in our human DNA. Deep down I think everyone wants to be part of a great story or mission. So having that story, that passion, is far more important than big salaries at the beginning.

....

MY NEW FRIEND TULA had tried to build his company all by himself. He didn't have a team; he had a lot of small investors that had lent him money and now wanted it back as they realised things weren't panning out as planned. Sadly, it was too late for him to restructure his business in any meaningful way; it was too far gone and at an early stage, that's difficult to rebound from.

I introduced him to a friend of mine who is an insolvency professional and could help him manage his creditors and investors. He told Tula to fire his accountant—an uncle whom he disliked, who was also chasing him for money that he had also lent him—and to slowly gather people around him who could help him.

I knew the pain he was feeling. It's not a good place to be and you don't sleep at night when people are chasing you. You know because when you wake up it starts all over again.

I was there many years ago when I started small marketing a company in Norwalk, Connecticut. We grew pretty fast and built up a team in the direct marketing business. We had a warehouse full of product and an office full of women answering phones. We built a business selling exercise videos to women over 50 with health problems. Jane Fonda was all the rage, but no one had targeted these older women. We hit a nerve and almost overnight, we were selling loads of videos out of a warehouse in

Bridgeport Connecticut. Then, we lost our single contract. It was painful. It was just me. No ground team.

I had people chasing me for money, suppliers threatening me, and the government looking for taxes. And of course, I'd saved no money, only bought a brand-new red Cherokee Jeep and a closet of nice clothes. Game over.

·······

BEING BY YOURSELF is a lonely place, and when you get into trouble without team support, you suddenly realise you don't have many friends. Like Tula, back in Bridgeport I wanted to be bailed out. That wasn't going to happen, and I had to learn the hard way. In hindsight, it taught me some valuable lessons. And while I had a new Jeep, I had no team. Only one client and people filling boxes of video tapes on a conveyor belt. So you need to look at your business and understand each facet of it and build teams around that. If I'd had taken the time to build a team, we could have probably pivoted in some way out of my mess.

To succeed at anything, you need ground support; all-hands-on-deck kind of people who make stuff happen. People who can carry out your visions and plans and execute the work. Later on, in Central and Eastern Europe, as things went on, I quickly had to learn how to delegate, mostly out of necessity. It was a blessing in disguise because it forced me to rely on others.

Besides, working with a team is more fun.

You do stuff together. You work hard and play hard.

You will spend more time with these people than with your family. Those at the core become closer than close.

At Ober-Haus, we did everything together—we celebrated together, had birthday parties in our offices, and went on weekends away. We hung out in saunas and jumped into freezing lakes together. We had awards parties where we gave out trophies for the best salesperson and best employee, and we had prizes for some goofy things as well. Everyone loved it. We did everything we could together.

In eighteen years of business with some 650 employees, I think I only lost five in total, and only two did I have to fire. I had somehow managed to get all the right people on the bus.

Your team should be people you like. And they should have skills you don't have, which if you're like me, means pretty much everything. You will know quickly if they blend in with others or if they are difficult. If they don't fit in, let them go, and find new people. Keep doing that until you put together the right team.

Get the right team on the bus!

I say this because you want your team to not watch the clock but to work hard and follow you. Like I said, you will probably spend more time with them than your family. So finding the right team is crucial to your success.

·······

WHEN I STARTED my first business in Estonia in 1992, my team consisted of my personal assistant, who was also my translator, and me. We really weren't doing anything extraordinary at that time; we were just learning and trying stuff out.

At meetings, someone would start speaking in Estonian, and I wouldn't have a clue what they'd said until my assistant translated for me. I was on the back foot from the very start, so for me, hiring people became a necessity. It wasn't a strategy about building a great internal team; like something I'd read in a book, it was about being able to function as best as I could. So instead of being involved in every aspect of the business, I learned to hire people to do things because I could not speak the local language. Then, in order to keep myself current, I met with my managers (who did speak English) on a regular basis each week. Calls at midnight were standard.

Besides your internal team, you need to build a team outside the company. I see this network of professionals as an extension of my business. These people are just as important as your internal team, and in some critical moments, even more important. Lawyers, architects, marketing and PR specialists, accountants, and the construction companies we worked with—these were my outside team members. I made sure I hired the best.

As an entrepreneur you need to network. You never know when all these people will come in handy.

·······

IN 1998, DURING THE RUSSIAN CURRENCY CRISIS, the banks suddenly stopped lending. My equity also dried up. I was right in the middle of an important big-box retail development for a German retailer. I was ten million euros from completion and half way there. The banks wanted more equity, and we didn't have it, and my partners in New York weren't giving it. In a last ditch effort I jumped on a plane and flew to MIPIM to meet my partners on their rented yacht and pleaded. After some cokes and crisps they said no. I was in trouble. So I asked for outside help. My go-to construction company had built four large retail centers for me in the past, and they had cash and resources.

I went and asked the hard question, cap in hand.

Fortunately, they financed me out of my predicament until I completed the project and could finally back-end the financing with the banks once the tenant was in. So think of all your suppliers, service professionals, anyone that you owe money to, but who rely on your survival as potential sources of cash. Anyone really, who has a vested interest is seeing you succeed. They will be there when you need them if they think they will benefit from your survival.

Even by slowing down payables, you can smooth out cash flow and suddenly find more cash in the bank just by extending a month or two. There is a well-known cash flow formula I think everyone should learn and apply; "Buy low, sell high, pay late, and collect early." Let that be your mantra. There's a book out there with that title; I've read it several times.

You never know when your external team will really bail you out.

THINGS TO THINK ABOUT

1. Recognise you don't fly to the moon alone. Entrepreneurs need a ground team. You cannot mentally and physically do everything yourself.

2. Look at your business and ask yourself what its most important components are. Pretend you know nothing (even if you do) and identify jobs to fill. You need key employees managing each of those areas, carrying out your vision and plans, and executing the work.

3. Find the right people to support you in each discipline—
    hire stars—both in your internal team and through a net-
    work of companies and professionals. Your team should
    be people you like. And they should have skills you don't
    have. Try to hire the best you can.
4. Reward your team and build camaraderie through work
    and play. Retaining and maintaining good relationships
    with your team is crucial for success.
5. Use your external providers, use the cash flow formula to
    create instant cash.

Chapter 9

THE LEADERSHIP MYTH

> *No man will make a great leader who wants to do it all*
> *himself or get all the credit for doing it.*
> —Andrew Carnegie

DON'T COMPARE apples to oranges. Entrepreneurs normally are not good managers. You don't want to be both, and you cannot be both if you want your business to succeed. So many people get this all confused, and I think it's a fundamental problem when starting, growing, and running a business of any size.

I like to think of myself as someone who develops a vision, a narrative around that, maybe knows the end game. Then my job is to execute that by sharing that vision with my team; investors, bankers, and customers and making sure things are getting done. In other words, I draft the wireframe; they help build it. I like to think of entrepreneurs as conductors of an orchestra. They can't play each instrument as well as the individual members, but they have the entire score in front of them and interpret the way to completion. In a nutshell; entrepreneurs create change; and managers make sure the change actually happens. I think it is impossible to do both well.

When I was building my business in Central and Eastern Europe, I was a not "a manager." There was so much I didn't know how to do, but I did know how to create interest around an idea, sell that idea, and build teams around it to execute.

Both aspects of the business are vital, both are important. In fact, they go hand-in-hand, and it doesn't work when you just have one or the other. They are two separate functions, carried out by different people. And you need to recognise the difference.

In any business, there needs to be one guy, one guy responsible for the sense of direction guiding the way, and accountable for everything. Avoid decisions by committee at all costs. That guy needs to know how to sell and manage people well. Not the individual processes involved. That person will also need a lot of smart managers by his side and a healthy pick-up team below his senior management group. These colleagues will work 24/7 for you if they believe and trust in you. No, we don't fly to the moon alone. And yes, we need help. Without those motivated and loyal troops, entrepreneurs would just remain garage band startups and never really get anywhere.

·······

MANAGERS IMPLEMENT SYSTEMS. They execute and try to improve efficiency in service and production. Good managers get the most out of people and processes. Great managers make life easy. You give them the plan; they make it happen. Entrepreneurs design the product. Managers build it and keep building it. They solve the problems. Entrepreneurs ask the questions.

I'll give you an example. I hate to travel. I like being at home at night, reading books, hanging around with the dogs and my family, writing, making lists, and just thinking. I'm surrounded by familiar stuff and it gives my head peace. It seems the older I get, the more this applies. When I travel, I feel unsettled and transient. I don't think well, and I feel tired and out of place. Living out of suitcase is something I really dislike.

To expand our business years ago, when we were opening offices and business in other countries, I realised I needed someone who liked to run around, show up at endless meetings and stay up late doing dinners.

I hated flying into Warsaw on a Wednesday, checking into some uncomfortable but pricey hotel, eating bad food then hitting all-day meetings in nondescript buildings, and running around in smoked filled taxis. Most of the CEE countries in the 90s and even 2000s were still grey, dark and nothing really worked. That's why we were there in the first place, of course, but I still disliked travelling around and it didn't make it any more fun for me. I always just wanted to get back home.

To help solve the problem, one of my colleagues, a younger version of me, loved to travel and liked going out to dinners and discovering new nightclubs and people he could chat up. That guy opened all of our offices in five countries. He was always on the road, and he loved it and was super good at it. On my own, I could never have done what he did. The good news was that I knew that.

Another example.

Early on, I found a bookkeeper at one of the businesses our bank was funding. They made furniture and the owner liked horses and wasn't around the business very much because he liked competing more than he did selling furniture. But his business was wildly successful. Back in the 90s, all these people in these Central and Eastern European cities wanted all the stuff they had never had before. Cars, TVs, furniture. And yes, modern houses and apartments to live in.

And his bookkeeper did all the work. I mean, all the work! She'd have all the loan docs prepared, all the spreadsheets and she negotiated all the terms of the loan agreements with the bank. She was a magician and super switched on. She also had really long legs and wore really short skirts which was really distracting at meetings. Distractions aside, she was super smart, and this guy had no idea how lucky he was to have her doing all the work while he played.

Of course, a few years later as our real estate company Ober-Haus was expanding rapidly, I needed someone to do all the financials because it was really taking too much time from me. So, you guessed it, I hired her. She became the most important person to me over the next 15+ years, and I didn't do anything without her being involved.

·······

AS A BUSINESS PERSON, I'm good at finding the right people to do the job. I know what the picture is meant to look like and where I want to get to, but I couldn't tell you how to mix concrete or service a hotel. That's not my job, and I hate details. I can do details, but I'm not the best at them. And I know that.

Years later, when I found myself turning around a country house hotel that I had purchased, I had to do details. Funds were low. I was in trouble, and I couldn't afford to bring in people to help me. I knew I'd be forcing myself to manage operations. I'm not made for that, and while I knew I could do it, I also knew I wouldn't do the best job of it. Eventually, I would need to bring in managers if I wanted to survive. Managers are specialists, and leaders are generalists—we're not wired for details.

Finally, after months of doing a lot of things I really disliked, I started bringing in the help I needed, and that made all the difference. Before that, my wife would say, "Just teach him to do what you would do," or "show her how to be more organised." All very easy to say, but it's like asking a duck to ice skate. Every day, I'd go and do my job, and I was miserable. I was a terrible manager. I knew I was wasting my time. I'd spend half the day thinking up ideas, when I really needed to be working in operations.

Also when I invested in a fast food chain years later, I witnessed the same dynamic at work. The owner would try to be helpful by running the register if the store was too busy, making purchases, working on menus, doing the marketing, working on fit-out with designers and architects, and trying to find new locations. Very impressive, but not the way to grow a business. Eventually we changed all that, and the business grew.

Remember, it's your idea, your vision, and your company. Lead. Don't manage.

THINGS TO THINK ABOUT

1. Decide if you will lead or manage. You do not want to do both, and you cannot be both if you want your business to succeed. Entrepreneurs inspire change; managers make sure the change happens.
2. As a leader, your focus is to create a vision, know the end game, and share that vision with your team, investors, bankers, and customers.

3. The other part of your time should be spent finding good people to manage operations. Managers make your life easy. You give them the plan; they make it happen.

4. Have regular meetings with your senior managers to make sure the pick-up teams are doing their jobs. You need to keep sharing the vision with your management team, and you must stay aware of what is happening in the team—both good and bad.

Chapter 10

THE IDEA MYTH

> *Everyone who's ever taken a shower has an idea. It's the person who gets out of the shower, dries off and does something about it who makes a difference.*
> —Nolan Bushnell

▌ **HAVE ABOUT TWENTY IDEAS A DAY.** Twenty great ideas. I'm sure of that! But they come and go. Ideas, like food, are perishable. And like food, they are super tempting. The menu of ideas can be like a visit to Sticks & Sushi in London; I never know what to order because the menu is thirty pages.

Ideas come in a blink of an eye, like a Eureka moment, and they hit us without warning. And most simply evaporate as fast as they came. Thankfully, by the following day, I've forgotten most of them.

Yes, everyone has great ideas, and I'm sure everyone can think of dozens that they think are billion-dollar ideas. I probably have thousands of "If only I had done that" moments—and that's just in one day.

Probably those ideas, like mine, are mostly impractical. One day, I may have an amazing idea about international money transfers, and the next day I'll envision how to do stocktaking for a fast food chain. Or how to create a peer-to-peer lending platform. The list really is endless.

Thing is, if I'm not somehow connected to my idea, or in those sectors already, chances are it will be extremely difficult for me to get any traction without investing significant time and resources. I'm not saying it can't be done, but it's a long-shot.

Ideas without any relevance to your personal circumstance I think, are a total waste of time.

Fact is, you really can't get to point B if you don't know where point A is. And you don't need to know much about point A right away either. But you do need to have some grasp of point A or somehow be associated with it. For example, I didn't know about hotels, but I did know a lot about real estate and about building. This allowed me to get into building and then operating hotels. Same with shopping centers and big box retail. Whatever direction our company moved in was a natural progression of what we were already doing somehow. It was a lateral move, creating another business silo under the umbrella of the business we were already in. You don't want to jump around all over the place.

·······

BACK IN THE 1980S, when I was about eighteen years old and had my first job on the Chicago Board of Trade, my buddy David and I would go down to the deli for coffee before going on the trading floor, and every morning we would get our hot coffee in those Greek-style paper coffee cups with the plastic lid on top.

One day, David ripped a v-shaped hole in the plastic top of the coffee lid so he could both cool it and drink it while keeping the lid on and walking. Suddenly, he stopped, looked at me and had one of those eureka moments. "Hey, wouldn't it be cool if all plastic lids had a flip-top!" he said grinning from ear to ear.

That said, sadly David nor I are billionaires from that billion-dollar idea.

We were eighteen-year-old kids with no money and just had one of those universal moments that happen to people all the time. We'd never invented anything, and we were clerks on a trading floor. We didn't know anything about anything at the time. So we didn't do anything with the idea. Today, of course, every plastic lid has a perforated hole. Someone made a billion. It sure wasn't us.

Great idea.

Yes, I wish I'd invented the flip-top lid, video real estate, YouTube, coloured flip-flops, virtual casinos and about a hundred other great ideas I've had over the years that have flown through my head at one point or another.

Ideas are universal. And I've got a hunch that for every idea we have at any given moment, there is someone else somewhere in the world having the same idea. Or maybe ten-dozen people for all I know. One of those people will somehow be connected and have the right circumstance to make it work. Everyone else will forget about it the next day or if not, never be heard of and will fail. Just think Bill Gates. He was writing code at 13, working in one of the only computer school labs in the country. There were others doing the same thing. We just don't know who they were. Bill had the advantage.

....

TODAY MY COMPANY PROVIDES capital to real estate development projects in Great Britain. My only credit background was helping to build that bank credit department years ago. Yeah, that's big stuff, but it was long ago, in a very different cowboy market, and most people who I deal with today weren't even out of high school at that time or even born. So, it doesn't count for much. That said, it does have relevance on a few levels.

The links that connect the dots between providing credit and real estate is the development experience I had accumulated, the financial management skills I had developed along the way, and the skills needed to build an organisation from scratch. Providing capital then doesn't become such a huge, out-of-the-box idea. It's a natural progression of all the things I did and connects all the dots. It's not like I'm manufacturing electronic bikes or children's clothes; two things I really know nothing about.

·······

IT'S REALLY THE UNDERLYING and surrounding circumstances that determine who makes it work and who has the ability to move forward with an idea at any given moment. Don't worry about it; one day the right idea will appear that fits the place you're at in your life, and you won't even know it's coming.

Fast forward from the days of riding my Schwinn in the cornfields of Illinois, watching malls and residential suburbs being built all around me, to writing business plans for Sergei; to setting up a credit department and working in a new bank and buying and flipping apartments. Those dots connected in ways I never would have imagined. Those dots led to building commercial retail and residential projects across Eastern

Europe, and now to providing capital for development projects. In hindsight, it looks like an A to Z. But it sure wasn't. It was a very zig-zagged path leading to one thing in the end. The one overarching idea was I really just wanted to build stuff.

One day, Margus walked into my office and laid a city map out on the table. "Here," he said, "is where we should build a grocery store." We had never done anything like that before. We knew nothing about building retail. And yet, that was the beginning of the shopping centers we built for the next fifteen years. One day before, I would have never imagined building shopping centers. I mean, for real? But then again why not? We were already in the real estate market, doing other stuff. So it was really just a step sideways and up.

Strangely, each of these ideas snuck up on me, slowly developing in their own magical way, until suddenly there was a confluence into one Big Idea. A lot of small stuff, a lot of small ideas, one at a time. I never went out and said, "Okay, we're going to be the biggest commercial retail guys in the market."

But when I finally started building shopping centers, I was already knee deep in the real estate business; having built a bunch of single units, moving to full buildings, and having started and expanded an advisory business. So we were already there, so to speak.

I was moving laterally within a business I was already in. Real estate was something I knew about and had already been drawn to. I wasn't suddenly designing women's fashion accessories.

If you start with one thing, it will eventually take you down the right path without you noticing. That's how ideas and how life works I think. Chances are, the business you want to start is related to something you know about, or are passionate about, or have been thinking about for some time. Steve Jobs studied graphics and design; he didn't go into fast food. When you take strides toward your vision, you'll come to know your arena pretty well.

Once you've decided and figured out the right idea mentally and thought about how to proceed by constructing and deconstructing the idea a few times with colleagues, you then need to start committing in a real way—and make an execution plan: What do you need? Who do you know who can help you? What should you do first? What kind of budget do you have?

Get all this stuff down on paper. Get it out of your head. If you don't like it, start again. Write down everything. Make a shopping list of things you will need, starting from day one.

·······

AS I WAS STILL MEETING and helping Tula liquidate his company, I also started researching Africa. Strangely, it seemed every Facebook and LinkedIn post I was reading featured startups in Africa, entrepreneurship, and team building. I was intrigued.

I also started following people on LinkedIn and Twitter and paying attention to current news in the different west African regions. One day, I read an article written by an entrepreneur and startup thought leader named John-Paul Iwuoha. He had written a book, *101 Ways to Make Money in Africa*, which was full of thought-provoking business Ideas.

He had founded a company called Small Starters and was doing a lot of blogging on entrepreneurship. So I started following him and sent him an invitation to connect. Then I waited. More ideas.

THINGS TO THINK ABOUT

1. Make a habit of brainstorming and let your ideas flow. You'll have many crazy ideas, but eventually a good idea will strike at just the right time.
2. Find what you enjoy doing or what you see yourself doing. Remember that the one idea is almost always one that fits with your skills or what you've been doing or are familiar with.
3. Construct an execution plan of what you need. It may take a few dozen times to get it all down because as you think it through and write, more issues will surface which you need to solve for.

Chapter 11

GET GOOD AT EXECUTION

> *No EXCUSES. No explanation. You don't win on emotion.*
> *You win on execution.*
> —Tony Dungy

I BOUGHT JOHN-PAUL'S BOOK about African business ideas and four days after I sent him a LinkedIn invitation. I saw he had "connected" with me, so I sent him an email. I gradually introduced myself; he did the same. I read his blogs, and he read mine. I thought it might be a good idea to meet, maybe in London. I messaged him about Tula and his story; I wasn't sure where any of this was really going, and just wanted to let it play out.

We agreed a meeting would be good, but he told me he was living in Lagos so we decided to Skype instead. That's the power of technology. I'm in London and he's in Lagos and we are Skyping. Today we use Teams, but whatever the technology, it blows my mind how small the world has become. Today, we can have remote meetings from anywhere in the world, and connectivity makes everything so much faster and more efficient. To be honest, it's hard to imagine working any other way these days.

In a matter of weeks, I'd moved from a chance meeting with Tula, to reading a blog on LinkedIn, to sending a message to Lagos to Skyping a new friend across the ocean. We talked about Tula's idea and the many ideas John-Paul had, but the real problem always came down to how to execute all these ideas.

What I've learned after chasing lots of shadows, is that at the end of the day, the key is not the million-dollar idea but the million-dollar execution plan that you build. Personally, if given the choice, I'll always take a mediocre idea I know something about and can execute well over a great idea that I know nothing about and will execute poorly. Do you bet on a great entrepreneur with a marginal idea, or a mediocre entrepreneur with an amazing idea? Jockey or horse? A lot of debate around that.

Of course, there's a fine balance here, but I think for starters I'd rather back a good management team who I know can get it done and who have been there before ahead of a great idea.

·······

THE KNOWING HOW and the execution are the single most important aspects of success in any business. Of course, you can always learn "how" but that takes some time and a lot of financial resources. So, as an entrepreneur, I try and hire colleagues who can get the job done, execute our ideas and ensure they get done. Steve Wozniak knew about computers; Steve Jobs didn't. Apple was only possible with both their skill sets.

Ideas, plus execution skills, equals success.

You can spend all the money and time you want on marketing and sales, building your digital platform, and public relations, but if the machinery isn't working properly, if you aren't paying attention to execution details, you might as well just close the door and go fishing. It's all a waste of money unless you can deliver real results.

One of my partners, a young guy who is amazingly smart, always says that our real job is solving problems and when all the problems are done, we can go home. Of course, every day we find new problems and things we didn't know about and need to know about. Good execution is about finding those problems, finding what works and what doesn't, and then doing that and getting rid of the shit that doesn't work. People too. Work through it, solve, and move on. There's always a problem to solve and to execute.

· · · · · · ·

IN 2011, I bought a country house hotel outside of London, close to where I lived in Oxford, I thought I could turn this rundown Tudor house into a cool place for people to come and spend some time. It was an amazing place and had loads of history and pedigree. I mean I was thinking how hard can this be? Just throw some money at refurbishing it, clean up the gardens and get the food right. No brainer. People will flock.

One day, someone was trying to get hold of me and had tried repeatedly to call me at the office at my hotel. Finally, exasperated, she emailed me: "I've been trying to call you all day and no one is answering the phone, please call me." I thought that was a bit strange. I had loads of people working at the hotel, so no reason the phone shouldn't be answered.

Curious, I walked out of the outbuilding where my office was and into the main house. I wandered down the cool stone-floored medieval corridor of the oldest part of the building and down the staircase into a fantastic Tudor-period main hallway. This was such a cool place I thought. What a lucky guy I am.

The hotel had twelve acres of beautiful topiary gardens and I had just built a tennis court and cleaned up the pool and could see myself lunching by the pool and having summer parties with friends. I was thinking, this is just great!

But as I walked down the corridor, I noticed it was strangely empty of staff. I saw no waiters. I kept walking. When I reached the front desk, no one was there. The phone was ringing. I'd just spent thousands of UK pounds on marketing, boosting ads on Facebook, writing blogs, and sending e-shots. Yet the cold reality was that the phone was ringing, and no one was answering.

I found half dozen people in the kitchen having lunch. Now that is bad execution. Clearly my fault.

· · · · · · ·

OVER THE LAST FIFTEEN YEARS, I've built and owned three hotels and one that only made it to the planning stage in Krakow, Poland. They dotted Central and Eastern Europe and were the first luxury, five-star hotels in some of those cities. We were one of the first people doing that in what was the former Soviet Union, so people came to us because there were no better places to stay. Anyone who was anyone stayed with us. I have two books of photos with rock bands like the Stones, Joe Cocker and his band, Sting, and even lessor known heavy metal bands; European heads of state and royalty. They came because we offered first class service and luxury fit-out in a market that was lacking both.

Back then, I was fortunate enough to hire German and

Austrian hotel managers who knew their stuff, and they put the locals through the paces of customer service and operations. Our local team was excited; willing to work hard because they were thrilled to have jobs at such prestigious hotels, so they never watched the clock. This was a massive opportunity for most of them and they were proud of their jobs; they actually cared about what the customers thought. They were extremely motivated to execute at a high standard.

Years later, when I bought that country house hotel in the UK the situation was totally different.

Fact. No one wanted to work. I just didn't get it. No one cared about service or quality; and most people were only interested in a paycheque and watching the clock. They were more worried about their vacation time than being proud of the work they were doing. That kind of mentality needs to go, it kills any hope of execution done properly.

In the end, it took having to start with a whole new staff, (mostly Europeans), who really wanted their jobs and were willing to work hard. I've had nineteen restaurants in London, and the story was the same there, too. Every time I hired local staff they watched the clock, and things floundered, but every time I hired Poles, Spanish, Italians, they worked hard and the business improved and ran successfully.

Bottom line, the Brits could learn a thing or two about customer service and hospitality work. There's a certain sense of entitlement that you really don't get from hiring Europeans for that kind of work.

Since execution is the single most important ingredient for success, you'd better make darn sure you have the right staff to make it happen. Hire people who want to work, are good at what they do, and reward them. Create a vertical ladder of opportunities for your employees, and train them relentlessly. If you don't know how, bring in someone in who does.

Think of all the businesses you know of. What makes the good ones stand out over the others? Execution. A lot of other factors come into play, but fundamentally, it all boils down to the execution. A hamburger is a hamburger at the end of the day, but think what McDonalds did in the early days when they transformed roadside burger stands. It was all about execution, time and time again.

If your employees aren't getting the job done, replace them. Don't be trapped by convention or guilt. Give all new employees a thorough try, of course. Train them. Start by being specific about what they need to do and if they struggle to do their job well because they simply don't know what they're doing wrong, bring in someone to help them.

If that fails, then there is only the door.

We had a guy we hired from a senior level position at one of the High Street banks to help run our credit side. He was meant to run all the customer due diligence checks for our business when on-boarding borrowers or developers we financed. We were all deal guys, great finance guys, great at structuring deals, great at knowing which were best deals and then creating the best in class deal memos and credit papers, but we were short on risk and credit skills so we hired him and paid a recruiter a lot of money as well.

After one month, I knew it was a mistake. He couldn't communicate and his presentation skills were dreadful. We brought in help and put him on probation. Everyone bitched about him, but no one had the nerve to just say he had to go. I knew he had to go, but I kept giving him chances, until he almost cost us a several deals.

You'd be surprised how many entrepreneurs get tied to ineffective staff because they like them or feel badly about firing them. After a while, there's a certain sense of guilt that takes over. Or sometimes you think it's too expensive to let them go. Actually, it's too expensive not to let them go. I've been in that spot many times, and I only have myself to blame for the shabby results. So I've learned to be quick about it. And the bigger you get, the easier it is to ignore some of these people, until one day you look around and realise half the people are costing you a fortune and not producing.

You're in business to create, build, and add value, no matter what it is. Don't waste your time with people who can't execute and get you to where you need to go. Only keep staff who are determined to work hard and care about success, and who are willing to work those long hours and learn.

THINGS TO THINK ABOUT

1. Execution is critical. You can spend all the money and time you want on marketing, building your digital platform, and public relations, but it's all a waste of money if you can't deliver.
2. Find people who can provide the skills you need. Only hire staff members who are eager and willing to work hard. Then pay them well and earn their loyalty.
3. Train your employees and give them the tools for success. Good employees and managers are determined to succeed. Encourage that determination by creating a vertical ladder of opportunities.

4. If employees don't want to work or don't care about service or quality, let them go. Since execution is the single most important ingredient to success, you have to ensure your staff is willing to make that happen.

Chapter 12

FRIENDS AND TURKEY DINNERS

> *If you like a person you say 'let's go into business together.'*
> *Man is a social animal after all, but such partnerships are*
> *fraught with danger.*
> —Brian Tracy

TULA WAS FACING A PROBLEM familiar to many entrepreneurs. In his quest to raise capital for his new venture, he had relied on friends, family, and his casual acquaintances. Most people think this is the logical place to start. And maybe in the beginning it is.

But it's not a good idea if it can be avoided.

Yes, sometimes it's the only choice, but from experience I think it's better to try and raise capital from total strangers or professional investors if at all possible.

Because almost all his investors were friends and family, Tula now faced the emotional pain of having let them down. When my mother lent me money to trade on the trading floor years ago when I was young and stupid, and I'd lost it, it put a terrible strain on our relationship and with my siblings later on. Of course, telling anyone that you lost money or need more is difficult, but telling your family you lost them money is a very difficult thing to do.

When you start losing your family's money, it's not easy to sit at the table with them over Christmas dinner. You avoid phone calls and contact. There is both regret and guilt. There is an uncomfortable silence around the relationship or a lot of arguing and silent blame.

Either way, not good.

Also, while you carefully think about the types of investors you choose, there is also the issue of how to structure an investment. A lot of first-time businesses start as partnerships, and while in the beginning it may seem like an excellent idea, chances are, maybe not.

Normally, partnerships are pulled together by people with complementary skill sets or, one has capital and the other has experience. On the surface, those complementary investments work well, but almost always one dominates the other. So, from the start, those attributes need to be identified and spelled out clearly in any agreement or else problems will arise.

Years ago, I bought into a startup fast-food company in London. It was owned by a young guy and who was basically running the show from the back of his scooter. It was a trend-setting concept, and I wanted in.

He needed capital to grow his business and also needed some expertise at helping with that growth. Me, I'd just exited from Central and Eastern Europe, and I was looking for something interesting with potential to do. Also, my wife was tired of me hanging around the house with nothing to do but repeatedly walk into the kitchen or her office. It was a perfect excuse to do something outside of my comfort zone and get out of my wife's hair.

Thing is, I had always been the majority owner and run my own companies. My outside institutional investors pretty much let me get on with things as they invested as joint venture partners on a deal-by-deal basis. Outside of the occasional phone call, meetings and the financial reports on each project, I hardly ever saw them.

But when I signed the deal with my new fast-food partner, I was entering into a relationship that was something completely different to what I had been used to. The way I thought about it was that in addition to being an investor, I was an equal partner, which meant I planned to head into the office every day.

Of course, as a former operating partner to some pretty big investors in my past life, I had a pretty strong opinion how things should be run operationally and how growth should be managed. So when I showed up for work in the following days, our relationship became a battle—a push and pull struggle culminating in some very painful moments. He just didn't want me around and felt that I overshadowed him.

I think he had always expected me to provide the capital and let him get on with things. I didn't see it the same way, and somehow in our eagerness to do a deal, we forgot to discuss what my involvement was going to be. I don't blame him, but I should have known better.

So our partnership was a disaster from the second day.

．．．．．．．

IN ANOTHER entrepreneurial episode I ventured into at about the same time, a good friend and I decided to buy a business together. Again, we did it as partners, because we were friends. Everything went great in the beginning, but when more and more money was required, my good buddy was unwilling to up his investment into the business, nor did he want to dilute his shareholding by allowing me to invest more on my own. So we found ourselves in a deadlock with no deadlock provisions to help us out.

What's even more crazy was that we were both professionals, and the money was not huge. In the beginning, we really just trusted our relationship to sort us out if any problems came up. But that's not what happened.

Our friendship, whatever it had been, eroded over an endless series of heated debates which we could not settle between ourselves without a lot of shouting.

I'd known this guy eighteen years. We'd had dozens of dinners, gone on vacation together and he was one of the first guests I invited to my farm in Argentina when I bought it. He wasn't my best buddy, but he was a buddy nevertheless and someone I liked and highly respected.

The sad part of it all was that falling out with him over a small business deal killed our friendship. Today, I have to ask, why did that even happen? What was the more valuable asset in the long run—the business—or our friendship? I know looking back that never should have happened, and it took years to get back on track. But it was never the same.

So no family, no buddies, and think of structure and problems from the beginning. And documents and agreements must foresee potential problems before they happen and have ways to resolve them.

·······

MY ADVICE is those hard decisions are ones you never want to make if you can avoid it. You never want to force yourself into having to make calls against people you care about.

In a partnership, there are two people; they always start

out well, but eventually each develop different agendas. Any partnership needs to think how disagreements will be handled, but even with an agreement in place, negotiating with someone you know is never easy at the end of the day. There's simply too much history that can get in the way.

You might think, "no way, that would never happen". And yes, maybe your friend is a great guy, or maybe you just want a buddy because you need some support, but when things go wrong or tough decisions need to be made, you need to be able to act quickly and execute change without lengthy discussions based on emotion.

All partnerships will eventually struggle with an eventual deadlock. Most occur as a natural progression of interests and objectives that change over time. So avoid pure partnerships, and don't do business with friends you want to keep.

·······

KEEP FAMILY AND FRIENDS for family and friend stuff. You want to eat dinner with them, talk about the kids, school and football. You want to pop over to their house for a coffee on Saturday morning and shoot the crap. You do not want to hide from them or fight with them.

So where do you go when you need capital? Whether you are starting from scratch, or your business is growing madly, you will always need money.

Thing is there is loads of capital out there looking for good ideas and management teams. It takes time, a lot of leg work and connections help, but you can raise that money from professional investors for equity and bank or private debt.

You will always need capital to fund cash flow, and for new opportunities. In fact, growth will eat through capital faster than slow sales. That's hard to explain to people that don't know how capital and cash-flow requirements work.

Also, it's good to bear in mind there's a big distinction between a private investor and an institutional investor.

If your funding requirements are small, say less than £20mm, or even in some cases even higher, chances are the institutional guys won't have an interest. Not only do you need size to get in the door, you will need a clear track record. Institutional investors are too busy doing deals, raising capital, and monitoring their portfolio investments and operating partners than to deal with a small startup, no matter how great the idea.

On the other hand, a private high net worth investor may be the best bet because normally, they do not have the resources to access good deals and are always more approachable and open to more opportunistic stuff. These could be guys who have money from a business exit themselves (most often are), or they could be from a Family Office with legacy capital. A Family Office can be either a single or multi Family Office that manages the wealth of multiple investors. They are not so easy to find, but if you do find them, they are generally more approachable.

Both categories invest for a living so they understand capital requirements, and how things can go pear-shaped. Mistakes are never easy to explain to anyone, nor is losing money, but they are probably cooler and more level-headed about it than your mother or family friends. And they can ultimately help with some sound advice because they want their investment to work out.

·······

ONE OF MY FIRST JOBS was as stockbroker for some small regional midwestern firm called Blunt Ellis based out of Milwaukee, Wisconsin. And my first clients were family friends. People that knew my dad mostly. I sold them the Blunt Ellis offerings that were shoved down our throats every day, and frankly, I had no idea if these were good deals or bad deals. We just needed to sell them.

Problem was, when they lost money (which they normally did) I felt personally responsible and guilty. These doctors and dentists came to our house for dinner. These trusting family friends were my clients and I couldn't sleep at night. It was the most terrible feeling and one of the worst jobs I think I ever had.

However, later on as I got better at what I did, I managed to get bigger clients and a few small-sized institutional investors. If we lost some money it wasn't a game changer and at least I wasn't distressed. I didn't like having lost money, but I realised these were professional investors; they'd already underwritten a portion of their portfolios to lose and it wasn't a personal thing. Food wouldn't come off their tables. Whereas if I helped a friend or family member invest a portion of his savings, it did hurt him if he lost—and by extension, it hurt me. That's the difference between family investors and professional investors. It's emotion vs a clinical approach.

When I bought out some of my joint venture partners after the Russian currency crises in 1998 and then again after 9/11 in 2001, I was able to buy those assets pretty cheap. They wanted out, it was nothing personal, it was a clinical decision based on things that had nothing to do with me or our business.

·······

FINALLY, DON'T EXCLUDE DEBT as an option. Debt can come from both from private investors, or from banks. By its very nature, debt is cheaper than equity. Simplistically, there is a rate of interest, and you need to pay it back at some point. Interest payments can be a drain on cash flow if there is too much leverage, but I'd rather pay a bank interest than sell away my shares any day. Debt has security over your business or assets, equity in its simple form does not.

Equity is the dearest thing in the capital structure and it's expensive. Don't give it away; don't share it if you don't have to, especially with friends and relatives. These are people you need to see every day and eat Christmas dinner with. Go watch a football game with them and get your money from the professionals and from banks.

THINGS TO THINK ABOUT

1. When you need capital, be clear about how much money you need now and, if possible, over the next five years.
2. If the amount is small, don't waste time trying to get in the door of Goldman Sachs.
3. Try not to structure a pure partnership, and don't do business with friends you want to keep. Falling out over business deals or debt kills friendships.
4. Start talking to professional private investors. Consider what professional investors bring to the table beyond equity—like experience, counsel, and connections with other experts.

5. Don't exclude debt as an option. Go talk to your bank. Ask if they have a business-growth lending department. Interest payments can be a drain on cash flow if there is too much debt, but it's usually better than selling a majority of your shares.

6. Hire a good corporate lawyer to draft any agreements.

Chapter 13

KNOW THE NUMBERS

> *Most years, if you were to ask me how much I make, the*
> *genuine answer is that I have no clue. I usually find out the*
> *answer to that question once a year, at tax time, when my*
> *accountant tells me.*
> —Simon Sinek

RECENTLY, I SPOKE AT an entrepreneur's conference at a well-known business school in Oxford. The room was full of experienced, middle-aged executives who were taking an entrepreneurial course for a week. Smart guys.

Some of them were there because they were looking to start their own businesses. Some were just curious. It was a well-heeled and well-educated crowd. I was only one of many speakers throughout the week, and my talk focused on start-ups. We talked about ideas, building a team, networking, and branding. Before wrapping up with exit strategies, we had a session on finance and accounting. I wasn't planning on spending too much time on it, thinking it would be super boring for this group.

At the start of the session, I asked how many people actually did their own personal accounting every month: things like reviewing their assets, their debt, and personal cash flows.

I have always done my own numbers, and for the last twenty-eight years can pretty much account for every penny, if

I need to. I think if you do this for yourself, it becomes easier to manage the business end of accounting.

What amazed me was that out of a group of thirty-five adult business people, only two raised their hands. I find this incredible. I was standing in front of a group of business executives who never did their own accounting. Yes, they paid the bills each month, and maybe based expenses on their bank balance. They may have had a sketchy idea of their future budget—but that was it. There was very little planning or asset management involved. I guess when you get a large steady paycheque every month, you naturally fit into a rhythm of spending that you become accustomed to.

But as an entrepreneur, there is no steady paycheque, or maybe no paycheque at all for a long while, so you really need to know your numbers pretty well or you're toast. Running out of cash is the worst sin.

I look at my personal records every week and do monthly accounts and budgets for myself and my business. It keeps me focused and helps me make wise choices. I can't imagine how to do it any other way. Especially as your business grows—you acquire assets and toys, repay debt, plan vacations, and deal with unexpected events. What if things slow down, and your business goes bust or cannot support you anymore? You can't afford to be blindsided by bad news. Black Swan events can take you out in a jiffy, and even the best managers probably don't plan for the unexpected. I'm a big believer in planning ahead for the unexpected and to have an idea of what happens "if". Even with all that, the unexpected can always be worse than you think.

········

THE LAST TIME I MET with Tula in our London cafe, I asked him to bring his accounts with him. Before putting his company into liquidation, I wanted to see how bad the future really looked for him before suggesting he pull the trigger. I was looking to see what assets, if any, were in his operating company and what he could salvage. Did he have any trademark rights? What was his goodwill worth? Was his brand worth salvaging?

Sadly, there wasn't much there, and no surprises, he wasn't able to explain any of it to me because the figures had been done by someone else—his uncle. He didn't understand the burn rate of cash he was going through. All he knew was that he was out of money, yet he was still producing and selling his product and creating more and more supplier debt.

With the fast-food chain I'd invested in years earlier, we had a similar problem at one stage. We had hired a corporate finance guy who was a buddy of my partner, and he was super convincing that everything was under control. So much so, I rarely probed and only saw the monthly reports. I really liked him, and he was super smart and is still a friend. But he was over his head, in my opinion. He was more of an entrepreneur and less of a CFO.

The problem became more apparent when we went to the bank for a line of credit to help with daily cash flow issues. Our sales were growing 24% year-on-year, but we were hopelessly always out of cash. The growth monkey was on our back and we needed a cash cushion to manage our growth or we needed to slow that growth down.

The problem turned out to be more or less a cash management problem and our CFO, who by the way was great in meetings and talking a good show, was not up to being a CFO in that he really didn't get the numbers and our bookkeeping system was a mess.

Bottom line know your numbers.

·······

IN MY FIRST YEAR OF RECOVERY, getting sober and off the crazy drugs back in 1987, I was confronted with the harsh reality of the financial mess I'd made of my life and the amount of money I'd actually wasted as I partied my way through New York. Really, I had no clue what I had done or spent.

I was receiving a pretty good salary for a twenty something year old and every two weeks on payday I allowed myself to be reckless with dinner, nightclubs, booze and drugs and then start again with the next paycheque. That meant, of course, that I was always out having too much fun and not being a responsible adult and paying attention.

The tidal wave of bills and expenses hit me hard when I finally lost my job. I had no savings, and no idea how to budget anything. I used to take bills and shove them into a shoebox and pay them as I went along. That was the level of my highly-organised financial administrative abilities at that time. I wrongly guessed that if I didn't see those bills, I could forget about them. Occasionally, I'd get phone calls, and I'd send off a check in the mail. When I finally lost my job, I stopped taking calls, just like Tula was doing now.

My girlfriend introduced me to a book written by a guy named Jerrold Mundis.[iii] It was about spending plans and

---

iii   Mundis, Jerrold. *How to Get Out of Debt, Stay Out of Debt, and Live Prosperously.* Bantam: New York. 1988.

how to get out of debt. It was a life-changing book for me! That girlfriend (who later became my wife) gave me the book after she discovered my shoebox and freaked out. That's when everything changed for me.

I blew through the book within a month. I worked out payment plans with all my creditors and started to feel in control, probably for the first time in my life. What a huge relief! I went back to answering the phone.

In those early days, I started carrying around a little book, and every time I spent money, I'd write it down. At the end of the day, I'd add it all up. Then I started taking those numbers and built a spreadsheet. Over time, that spreadsheet provided me with history. I could see figures represented as percentages of the total. I finally knew exactly where I was spending. I could determine if I was spending too much money eating out, on clothes, or on groceries, or even if I should be spending more in any of those categories. After a few months, it gave me a picture of who I was as a person at that time.

I don't carry around that little notebook anymore (although I think my wife would like me to—she hates how I like to spend money), but I pull all the numbers from my online bank statements. I still go through the monthly numbers, and I have a cash flow chart that covers over twenty years of history. I also have a schedule for net asset value, credit cards, and debt, with rates and payment dates.

Without these tools, I wouldn't have a clue about where I was or what I could or couldn't do. My guess is, if you're not doing that at home, you're probably not very good at it in your business. Like Tula or the executives at the conference, without that kind of financial control, you're just guessing,

THINGS TO THINK ABOUT

1. If you don't do your own personal accounting, start now. There's no substitute for tracking your income and expenses personally. It keeps you focused and helps you make wise choices.

2. Keep track of all your expenditures for one month. Put them in a spreadsheet and create a forecast for the next month. Create a net asset value page, which shows your assets less costs, plus uplifts less debt.

3. Do this every month and build an annual cash flow chart. This is a powerful tool for business planning, and it allows you to gain wisdom from seeing the effects of past choices.

4. Make sure you do it for your business and relish the knowledge you gain by studying the numbers and make wiser choices because of that knowledge.

CHAPTER 14

BUILDING A BRAND

> *Your Brand is what other people say about you when you are not in the room.*
> —Jeff Bezos

THINK RED BULL, Coke, KFC, Apple, Nike. Big brands. They conjure up images and thoughts and build customer awareness.

Your product or service is important. It needs to make sense and fill a need or solve a problem, or to create a need people don't even know exists yet. The numbers behind that product or service are important, profits are important, and cash flow is important, but how you position your offer is key; people will be drawn to you because of your story, the brand, the image you create and portray.

Messaging your business philosophy, product and theme is a constant process. It takes time and effort and it needs to be done correctly, or it's a waste, but it must be done. You always want to be front and center as much as you can be.

When building your business, you need to turn your vision into a business, and then your business into a brand. Think of impressive brands you know. You picture the brand, the logo, before you see anything else. Just driving by and seeing the Golden Arches triggers hunger for a double cheeseburger, shake and fries.

In today's digital age, we can gain more traction reaching out to potential customers than ever before. We have access to people's attention across the planet. Our marketing channels are bigger than they have ever been and have opened an entire world of possibilities.

The downside is that there is so much noise trying to grab your attention at the same time that our attention span lasts no longer than a minute. Your product or service somehow needs to grab people's attention and get above the noise in your sector. And that still takes time and resources. Both human and financial.

But gradually, you need to stand out—or you will be swallowed up like a drop of water in an ocean. And you need to be able to do that in whatever country or sector you're in.

·······

A BRAND CAN and sometimes does lead the business; in fact, it can even be bigger than the business itself. When we established our property company in 1992, we created a name and logo that did that. As we built our business across different countries, that brand helped us look bigger than we were.

People need to identify with the brand, to see it in their mind's eye, to recognise it in less than a second and it needs to mean something. If you can do that, you've added tremendous value to your business and set yourself for rapid growth. And when it's time to exit the market, it's that brand, the idea behind it, as much as anything else, that buyers will be purchasing.

So how do you rise above the noise? A name, a look, a colour or a story. I'm assuming you have a decent product or service but besides that, you need to shout. What can stand out to represent you in a crowded marketplace? You need to grab attention, and it needs to reflect who and what you are. If you are lucky, you might stumble on it one night while watching TV, or you might have to get a brand consultant to help squeeze it out of you. Eventually, it will come.

Today you can write articles, blogs, do podcasts, create videos, post on YouTube and buy multi-channel media. There is always email marketing and digital sales funnels you can explore. The choices can sometimes seem endless; and they are. So, start by knowing exactly who you are talking to and go granular. Start there and build from that. My advice is, don't throw money out everywhere because you will have no real impact and you will burn through loads of cash for no reason or result.

But whether you spend a load of money, or are simply sending out flyers, either way, you will need something unique and attention grabbing to make yourself visible. And once you have figured out what that is, build on that.

And try and get some help if possible.

Maybe you are not a great marketing guy, so trying to save money by doing it all yourself in the beginning may actually cost you more in time as well as in cash trying to figure it all out. Best if you keep to what you know and get some help if you can. Be selective, maybe hire an agency that can help you get the word out. You don't need to know how to do that. You need to make sure others communicate your vision in the best way possible and there are loads of people who do just that.

·······

IN 1993, I WAS RENOVATING one-off single apartment units and renting them out. Nothing big, just one at a time, and super small stuff. I had a few people working for me, and we were making a decent return renting and flipping stuff—enough to pay the bills and then some. To be honest, we really weren't doing anything that anyone else wasn't doing in our space. Maybe we did it a bit better, but that's about all.

One night, as I was watching TV and making notes in my journal, I unconsciously started writing my name and my wife's last name: Oberschneider and Hauser. I found myself combining the two names and drawing an ancient crest in the middle. The result was the name Ober-Haus, and it was an epiphany moment that changed my business for the next fifteen years. "Ober" means "Head" or "Top" in German, and "Haus," of course, is "house." Literally in German, the name means "House of Lords, or "Top House".

The beauty of that name was that all these small Central and Eastern European countries spoke different languages and had different cultures, but at their core, they were all historically Germanic. My competitors all had local, bizarre-sounding names that, while good in one country, could not transfer to other countries. The name Ober-Haus translated well in every country. It was perfect for a cross-border real estate company. I recognised it almost instantly and built our business around that theme. And for a long time that brand was our advantage to roll out a professional advisory business across multiple countries quickly.

We took that name and created a brand with brand guidelines to follow across the countries we expanded into and it worked. I kept thinking, Golden Arches. Where people saw our logo and name, they knew exactly what we did. It allowed us to grow where others could not get traction. That brand became recognisable everywhere we went. Not surprisingly, our brand actually became bigger than our business and helped us grow. Later on, when I sold that business, the buyer paid a premium for that brand.

·······

TODAY, AS I THINK ABOUT how we leveraged off our name, I'm looking at my phone, and I see hundreds of messages on social media. Hundreds of images and blogs to read. The trouble with the speed and breadth of social media and the digital age today is that there is just so much of it. Most of it is just bullshit and it comes fast. I mean, how on earth do you know what is real or not? You can spend hours just trolling through stuff, and at the end feel exhausted as well as disheartened.

Call me dinosaur and maybe I just don't get it. Maybe I've missed the whole media entrepreneur thing because I'm not tech savvy enough—but having wasted enough time myself on trying to stay "current" I've come to the definitive conclusion that almost all the information being pandered about is a total waste of time. Good marketers now have a global universe to work from and they take advantage of people. I'm kind of glad we didn't have all those media channels years ago because it would have made building our brand more competitive.

·······

MEETING MY NEW Nigerian author friend, John-Paul through the internet, reading blogs, and exchanging ideas across the world is mind-blowing. The power of technology and marketing tools is making our lives move faster and gives us loads of choices. But whether you are doing it digitally or making cold calls and putting up posters, building any brand takes time, and you need to be consistent with your messaging.

The formula, after all, is pretty simple—when starting a business, find some aspect of it that uniquely identifies you, that distinguishes you from the rest of the market. It could be your product, it could be your business ethos, it could be the language you use to target your audience. Maybe it's all those things.

Broadcast that element on a consistent basis every day until your brand somehow is known. Generally, the key to building a strong brand is to provide some kind of pleasurable experience or solve a distressing problem for your customers. Your brand needs to convey that people will get either pleasure or a solution from you.

THINGS TO THINK ABOUT

1. Think about what you do. Clarify your product or service. You need to turn your vision into a business and your business into a brand that stands out in an ever-increasing larger world.
2. Remember, people have short attention spans. Grab their attention and get above the noise in your sector.
3. Look at the competition and consider how crowded the market is.
4. You need people to identify with the brand, to see it in their mind's eye, to recognise it in less than a second. If you can do that, you've added tremendous value to your business and set yourself up to grow rapidly.

5. Build that brand into everything you do. Broadcast it on a consistent basis until you build recognition in the market.
6. Start small.

CHAPTER 15

THE IMPORTANCE OF BASKETS

The wealthy are always looking ahead. The less wealthy are thinking about Saturday night.

—Anonymous

IF YOUR CORE BUSINESS is a good one, it probably has more legs than you think. After a while, you will see product areas where you can vertically extend and market sectors you can horizontally shift into that you may have not seen before. Business is about solving problems, and as you solve one, you will find more, which will invariably lead to those verticals.

You'll quickly discover opportunities to expand what you are already doing in your core area into related businesses, which gives you diversity and potentially, multiple sources of income and value. Entrepreneurs are always looking ahead at the possibilities. They connect dots and lines where others don't see them.

Of course, your first core business is your most important asset and where you will probably be making most of your money. This is the business that will fund other ventures, and make or break you; so all your focus should be on building a team and a brand and rolling out that core product or service first. And that's exactly what you should focus on. Dashing off and chasing other ventures too early will hurt your core business and dilute your resources. So, make sure the main business is in motion and running well before darting off in some lateral direction.

At some point, though, you will see that there are other aspects of your business that can be divided, or at least segregated, into separate businesses. That's where it can get really interesting.

·······

AS I READ John-Paul's book, *101 Ways to Make Money in Africa,* I got lost in the world of possibilities. The book is full of ideas. John-Paul is passionate about African entrepreneurism and using it to drive growth on the continent. My problem, of course was, I wasn't in Africa, I was reading blog posts.

But with a population of over one billion people, how can you not be excited? Africa is a tempting arena. And it's not just its sheer size and population that makes it exciting—it's full of natural resources, human capital, impressive talent, and consumers; all at a very early stage. To most investors and entrepreneurs outside the continent, Africa is still a virgin market and a dangerous place. There is uncertainty, massive corruption, terrorism, and, in some parts, life remains cheap. It reminded me of what people used to say about Russia and the former Soviet Union countries: danger, car bombs, Russian mafia. But if you can get your head around all that, below the surface is huge potential. What is really lacking in Africa is a knowledge base of business skills. But that too, is changing rapidly.

John-Paul and I agreed to Skype more often. I had read his book and was full of questions. I thought that while Tula's product may not have worked in London, he should explore his product as an African business, and John-Paul thought it was an amazing idea. But there were problems to sort out.

What I discovered in our conversation was that while resources, and a growing market of consumers, made Africa a virgin market, the infrastructure for production was abysmal. As one of the major growers of fruit, for example, Africa is also one of the largest importers of oranges and bananas. Not because it doesn't produce enough, but because of a lack of road infrastructure, collection, storage, and processing. Fruit gets picked and then is left to rot. One idea led to another problem that led to another idea; herein lies the problem. Too many rabbits to chase!

And while there was plenty to do and trying to solve many of these problems would only lead to other problems, I realised that I was out of my depth and it would be a waste of time to get involved.

It's tempting to chase rabbits, but there is an old Russian proverb that says "if you chase two rabbits, you don't catch any." I think that makes sense. Focus on one thing, do that well and then let what you are doing guide you to doing more related things in a sector you already know and feel comfortable in.

·······

WHEN I WAS RENOVATING apartment units, I needed someone to source me on-going deals, and then I had to manage them after they were completed. Of course, I initially did manage them myself, but I also realised that I was at the point where I needed more help. Basically, I set up a management service company for myself. That was an organic progression that allowed my small core business to keep growing.

It became apparent afterwards that other, small-scale developers and property owners might like to use a management service too. That was really the start of our asset management business. It was kind of a no-brainer and corresponded to what we were already doing, anyway. So we built a property management business because, first I had to. That was the beginning of Ober-Haus Real Estate Advisors. It started slowly with one office, then over the course of 18 years spread across five countries; first for residential and then, as I built shopping centers, for commercial properties as well to 35 offices across the region.

As our business grew (and we were selling loads of homes to people), I found that we often had clients who didn't fit the lending criteria of the local banks. Especially in '98, after the Russian currency crisis when most banks froze up for a while. I knew the clients were there, and I could sell so many more homes if my clients had financing in place. Naturally, as we wanted to increase sales, we wanted to find a solution to the problem of lack of financing.

So that was the beginning of our mortgage company; we raised money and we would help our clients buy homes, and eventually we helped the banks by selling them our loans. I effectively became a loan origination business for the banks and markets shifted, selling off syndicated loans to the very same banks that wouldn't give these people credit in the first place.

By 2008, we had a retail and commercial real estate agency business, a residential and commercial property management services company, a mortgage bank, a property development company, and hotels. Every one of these were separate businesses, each with different services and priorities, but they all flowed out of the parent business, Ober-Haus Real Estate Advisors, with real estate being our core. One thing led to another just naturally.

The beauty of this, of course, is that when it was time to exit we had a pretty big basket. By 2006, we started selling down one at a time and were selective. The last thing I sold was the commercial retail portfolio.

At some point, you might feel that your company has achieved its potential, and you will have the luxury of being able to pick and choose which bucket to keep and which one to sell. Separating your business into different baskets multiplies your options and most often, they are more valuable as separate units.

THINGS TO THINK ABOUT

1. Your first business is your most important asset, so focus on building it and strengthening your brand. Don't get sidetracked chasing too many rabbits.

2. Watch for services and products related to what you are doing where there's an opportunity to provide a much-needed service or product. Start providing these new services and see if that branch of the business takes off.

3. As you grow, divide those services into separate businesses. Separating your business into different baskets multiplies your options and gives you the opportunity long term of picking and choosing which ones to keep and which ones to sell.

CHAPTER 16

WINNING AND LOSING

> *Even a mistake may turn out to be the one thing necessary to a worthwhile achievement.*
> —Henry Ford

AT SOME STAGE in the game, you may simply want to sell out. Maybe you've had enough, maybe you feel the timing is right, or maybe someone approaches you with a Godfather-like offer you simply can't refuse. Whatever the reason, think about it hard and speak to people, because while building a business can take years to do and to get right, once you exit, it's done. Game over and it will never be the same.

I've heard and been part of a lot of intelligent debate about exit strategies. Should you have one in place from the beginning? I'm not sure. I agree that you need an exit narrative for your investors who will want some idea of when they can get their money back, but when starting out, I'm not sure that it's really relevant. In reality, as you build your business solving multitudes of problems, one after another, what you end up with may be entirely different than when you started. In other words, things evolve with time.

When I started building those one-off flats to rent, I had no idea whatsoever what the future had in store. I had no vision of building a cross-border advisory business, no idea I would build commercial retail or build and operate a bunch of hotels.

No idea. And because of that, raising capital was difficult in the beginning as it always is, because investors know that. But after you're around for a while, even if you change strategy, you finally get it right. That's when things begin to take off. It takes years in most cases, and of course that's when raising capital becomes easier.

So deciding what your exit strategy is day-one is not going to be realistic.

·······

TULA MET WITH the insolvency guy I introduced him to, and he had to face his family and friends and tell them his decision. This was not the exit anyone wanted to hear about. It was the hardest thing I think he had ever done, and he knew that, at least for a while, they would probably be upset and refuse to speak with him. A forced exit is not a good exit plan.

Getting it wrong and having to sell for what you can is painful. Hopefully, no one has to go through that, but in reality, if you're not out there trying, you're going to get it wrong once or a few times so be prepared and catch it early, if you can.

When I was a trader on Wall Street, I learned a valuable lesson from a great floor trader on the NYSE. I worked for him and his partners. I was young and pig-headed when it came to losing trades. "Cut your losses short, and let your winners run . . . the trend is your friend," Herby used to tell me every morning as I went out the office door to the trading floor.

Thing is, most investors do the exact opposite. Like I did, and sometimes still do. It's the same in business. At least when you are trading, the pain of being wrong is quicker. You know instantly. Businesses take longer to bleed, and you might die a slow death, like a frog in a boiling pot. Tula was a frog in the pot. And as the water was boiling hot, he was still posting Facebook ads and blogging.

Tula's investors and family would forgive him eventually, and it was better to get it over with. He had turned to me for a loan, and I refused. Lending him more money wasn't the answer. His original business idea might have been a good one, but he had executed it poorly, and now he was under a huge weight of debt. There really was no way out of this for except to close down the business.

If you are luckier than our friend Tula, you will have founded a business you are proud of and one that has value. It makes a contribution, and you've built a strong team. Any working business has value, and someone will want it, since most people don't want the pain of building anything. There are a lot of investors out there that will just pay the price. It's like anything; if it has value, someone will want to buy it.

· · · · · · ·

IN 2007, JUST BEFORE THE FINANCIAL CRISES, I was lucky to be approached by a group of Finnish private equity investors who wanted to buy one of our core businesses. They wanted to bolt it on to their Scandinavian advisory service business, based out of Helsinki. That telephone call triggered a memory jog back to my sauna buddy Elvis and the lights flashed. Thing was, I was super comfortable and really had never considered selling.

At the time, we had several baskets of businesses that were doing well: a commercial retail and a residential and commercial development company with a fair amount of land banked, a hotel business, a mortgage company and a pretty wide-reaching real estate advisory business. Each of these businesses threw off a fair amount of cash, and by 2007, I never really had to worry about money. I had two farms in Argentina, a house in Buenos Aires, a flat in London, a summer cottage and my house in Tallinn, Estonia where I was based. I had built a huge network of contacts over 18 years and could pick up the phone to joint venture partners and banks and get funding for almost anything I wanted to do. Life was pretty good, and I was in my sweet spot, one that had taken me many years to find.

The problem was I was bored. I had allowed myself to be distracted. Big mistake.

I had built a nice little machine but I couldn't see the road ahead of me. And while my network was large, I really didn't talk to anyone about my business. Looking back, I was pretty isolated in my own head and my own world. I couldn't see the future and had hit a plateau of complacency and comfort. My senior managers were really running the business at that point.

That call from the Finns was more of a well-timed convenience than a well thought-out exit strategy. I took the call and the meeting, and the rest is history. For the next year, I worked at teeing up all my businesses and sold them one by one, including all my land banks. While my motivation for selling was seriously wrong, my timing was epic.

One week after I'd sold the last of our businesses, the markets around the world crashed and I was out. At the top, and I was suddenly super liquid. It was a Forrest Gump kind of moment. It came out of nowhere. Wrong reasons, great result.

········

WHEN YOU THINK ABOUT IT, the math is pretty simple. If you had a hundred dollars to invest and you minimised each loss to only ten percent, you could trade a hundred times before losing it all. A hundred times at anything is a long stretch.

Chances are, if you were disciplined enough to do that on every trade of venture in your asset allocation, eventually you would be right, and the winners would make you enough money to cover your losses. And if you were smart enough to pyramid on your winners and add to them as they grew, you could even multiply your gains more than tenfold.

Thing is, most of us do the exact opposite.

Entrepreneurs become attached to their businesses. They had a reason for starting them in the first place, and they struggle to admit when they are wrong. So they hold on, and continue to throw good money after bad. They always think their losers will turn around, and they usually don't.

For years, the hotel I bought in England haemorrhaged money, and I thought I could turn it around. I threw more money at the problem. I let hubris cloud my thinking because I had been successful so many times before, I thought I could adjust things and succeed this time. But the circumstances were different this time, and I couldn't accept that I was wrong. Basically, I ended up working for the bank for free, trying to save this asset and eventually, I ended up liquidating it and losing way more than I should have. It was a waste of time and energy. Losing takes its toll, both emotionally and financially. It's better to stop early, regroup, and start again rather than trying to prove something. Being stubborn doesn't make you smart. Pigs are stubborn, and they get slaughtered. I've been a pig a few times in my life, so I know what that feels like. Don't be a pig. Ask yourself these questions:

1. Are you losing money?
2. Are you emotionally tied to your decision?
3. What would be the consequence of getting out?
4. What would be the consequence of staying in?
5. Are you being honest?

If your business isn't making money—if you must constantly subsidise it with more funding—don't fool yourself, your investors, or your bankers into thinking it will come around. Be brave and honest. There's no harm in being wrong and failing. If it's not working, chances are it won't. In life, in business, in equity and futures trading, just get the hell out before the failure becomes spectacular. On the other hand, if you've been right all along and things are swimming, someone will come and take you out at some stage.

But think carefully about the reasons and what comes next. There's always the high of being right and exiting, but then there is the "what's next?" moment. It's almost the most important question to ask.

THINGS TO THINK ABOUT

1. Know how much you are willing to lose on any venture and stick to that commitment.
2. When you reach your limit, get out. Losing takes its toll, both emotionally and financially. It's better to stop early, regroup, and start again rather than endure a lingering death.
3. Don't make excuses. People become attached to their businesses, so they hold on and continue to throw good money after a bad idea.

4. Be honest with yourself, your investors, and your bankers. It's better for everyone to know what's really going on. This builds trust, and it's the right thing to do. It's not a failure to be wrong and shut down your business. The only failure is not getting out when you should.

5. When the opportunity comes along, you may want to take it and run. But you also need to think where you're going to run to.

CHAPTER 17

IT'S ALWAYS DARKEST BEFORE DAWN

You just never know what lurks behind the corner.
—Anonymous

LIKE ANYTHING IN LIFE, shit just happens out of the blue. As prepared as you might think you are, somehow, just for kicks, it seems life will throw you that curve ball at the last minute—almost as if life were seeing if you are truly awake and worthy.

And like anything in life, especially in business, you are always striving to close, making a decision, always trying to get a result. If everything would only just go our way, it would all be perfect.

The thing is, you're always learning; and if you're learning, it must mean you're getting bigger and growing and therefore ultimately pushing the boundaries of what it is you really do know. Which means that while it seems that life has thrown you a curve ball, most probably that curve ball is from your own pitch. Those curveballs life throws at us are direct or sometimes subtly indirect consequences of something you didn't do or know enough about to plan for or in fact something you did and need to pay the consequences for. You just got to own up to it, solve the problem again, find a new solution again, and do it quickly.

You will find time is your biggest enemy. Time is like an equity option and all equity options lose value the closer they get to expiration. All options waste in value. So in the beginning when you are young and immortal, time seems meaningless and in great abundance. There is plenty of it around. You spend it freely; you are far from the expiration date. But as you get older, the strike price gets further away and the premium on that option starts evaporating quickly.

Same in business.

When you start down the road of building something there is the appearance of time. But as you get started, every choice, every move you make, each with its own consequence, becomes a race against the clock. Tula found out the hard way, time was his enemy too. Today time is my enemy and it is my greatest asset.

·······

NOTHING GETS DONE BY DEFAULT. At the end of the day, anything worth getting is worth the effort—no matter how hard.

"Hard" is the operative word here!

Today, more than ever, there is way too much expectation on quick results and instant gratification. With fast news and social media, our focus has been shifted to achieving end results quickly and getting all the toys now. Real planning, setting goals and then actually actioning them, making mistakes and then making more mistakes and course adjusting only to make more mistakes, seems to be old-fashioned.

We expect ourselves and our efforts to be rewarded immediately and when the going gets tough, instead of the "tough get going", we think something is wrong or we quit and try something totally different.

What we fail to realise at every stumbling block is that the answer might just be around the corner if we give it one more try. Or maybe two or three more tries, or more even. We give up too soon. Believe me, there is always one more go inside you that you need to dig deep and find, even when the shit just keeps on coming. My partner, who likes to remind me of all the stuff I shouldn't do which mostly annoys me, makes this point. And he's right; Nothing Happens by Default.

Back in 1998, just as the Russian currency crisis hit with far-reaching consequences, I was halfway through building a large retail outlet and needed to draw down funds from the bank, as well as my investors, for the next phase. The banks wanted my partners to put up more equity and my partners refused to provide further funding and wanted the bank to provide more debt. It was a crazy situation and it appeared that I might have to let this project default.

I had a lot invested, and for my institutional partners this would be an unfortunate situation, but with $3 bn in assets, this small project in Estonia wouldn't make much of a difference. For me, the loss would be huge. Nuclear! Everything I had built up since the beginning was in that project and letting it go would be total devastation to say the least, not to mention I'd ruin my reputation in the market with my banks.

I even offered my partners more of my equity. They said no.

This was a defining moment.

I had really no idea what to do, but then it hit me.

I'd approach everyone who had a vested interest in getting this thing done. I probably broke every rule in my shareholder agreement at the time, but I borrowed from my anchor retail tenant, my contractor and all his subcontractors. They knew it was better to finish the project than leave a hole in the ground. I had to push, and I had to push hard and fast. I had to ask questions you feel uncomfortable asking and I had to break rules. WTF, I had no choice.

In the end, we finished.

The anchors moved in and the banks stepped up after the development risk was gone and stumped up the cash for me to pay everyone back. Even my partners were happy, although I had breached our agreement. In the end everyone got paid, and my net worth increased even more.

Nothing happens by default. You need to make shit happen. It doesn't happen any other way.

As you go out there and start something new, there will be a host of challenges that you will never be able to foresee. Agreements will be broken, things will happen, and it's at that defining moment you need to dig in and make it happen no matter what.

It's all part of the journey and there's really no turning back. Just remember and take this on board to make the journey easier; *the curve balls that life throws at you are normally of your own making. You just need to keep your head up and don't look down. Solve the problem, let go of expectations, and move on.* Everything will be okay.

THINGS TO THINK ABOUT

1. Be prepared for curve balls; shit happens when you least expect it, so learn to take sudden shifts in stride.

2. Use unexpected events as opportunities to learn. Solve the problem.
3. Nothing gets done by itself. Even with a team of people helping, you need to make sure stuff is getting done.

CHAPTER 18

LIFE AFTER EXIT

> *There comes a time in every life when the past recedes and the future opens. It's that moment when you turn to face the unknown. Some will turn back to what they already know. Some will walk straight ahead into uncertainty. I can't tell you which one is right. But I can tell you which one is more fun.*
> —Phil Knight

HOPEFULLY, after a lot of hard work, solving a lot of problems, sleepless nights, and day-to-day uncertainty a day will come when it's the right time to sell. It may be because you've been offered a silly price, or maybe you've had enough, and the right opportunity comes along. Maybe you sell down all, or maybe some, and step sideways to let some new blood and money into the business. Whatever the reason, nothing will ever be the same again. This is the part not many entrepreneurs have thought about or plan for.

When we are building something, we are too focused on the problem in front of us, scrambling to stay afloat, and trying to expand our reach—laterally and up and down stream. If we're lucky we get to build lots of baskets of businesses and revenue streams off of our core. And if we are really lucky, those revenue streams allow us the luxury to do things we only dreamed about and live an exceptional life.

But there is an if . . .

That's if the machine stays turned on!

Once the cash machine is turned off, a new life will begin, and if you have not planned for this carefully, you can easily go rudderless for a long time.

Selling out my businesses was probably one of the highlights of my journey. For a brief moment, it was an amazing feeling. It is the moment when you crystallise everything you've worked for and it confirms all of your efforts. It's all those years of smaller steps, bigger steps, and culminating in one single quantum moment. It is the big picture moment, the one you hang on the wall and stare at occasionally. There is no denying it if you've made it this far; you deserve every penny of it.

But there is a "but" . . .

The thing is, when you exit, all those people who were like friends and family, people you worked with for years will one-by-one, eventually disappear from your life. The phone stops ringing after a while and people are busy doing their own stuff. You kind of become slightly irrelevant when you leave the arena.

Hanging around the house, going on tons of holidays and exploring new hobbies is all good stuff and loads of fun, but it gets super boring for someone who's used to working like a madman, and for someone who is used to his phone calls being answered promptly even at midnight. Once you sell out, you become a different person; you are suddenly someone else.

·······

SELLING MY BUSINESS in 2008 was my Forrest Gump moment. We had ridden the global liquidity wave from 1992 until April of 2008 and had seen cap rates fall in emerging markets from 19 percent to 5 percent. That kind of yield compression will never happen again in our lifetimes. It was a moment in time, and some of us were incredibly lucky to be a part of it. Of course, with hindsight, it's easy to look back and say this.

That payday might well be the best day in your life, and the day after might well be the worst day if you're not prepared and have thought about it. Taking a few months off to reward yourself is fine. Indulge a bit. Enjoy. But then get back to work.

If you disappear, too much time passes, and the world moves on and the momentum you had built up will slowly come grinding to a halt . . . without a sound. That is exactly what happened to me, and it's extremely painful to go through.

After ten years, most of the people I had done business with had moved on, and the younger generation had no idea who I was or what I had done. One year turns to two years, to three, to four and ten and pretty soon you're a goner. And starting and building a new business again is extremely tough, so you don't want to do that.

The perverse thing about any successful exit is that most successful entrepreneurs sell at the peak of their careers, and only then realise they still have an entire lifetime ahead of them.

I had never thought about was what was next. A pile of cash is only that, a pile of cash. Numbers in a bank account or two. There is really no value to it unless you then use it again to create more value. And a pile of cash is super easy to spend. Burning through capital on things that don't produce is generally a bad idea. And when the machine is switched off, it's probably wise to hunker down, and look at how you've been spending and what you're going to do with what you have accumulated.

Sadly, I found out how easy it was to spend money. And I did it like I was some Columbian drug lord. And when you do that without putting it back to good use, you are heading down a rabbit hole.

I think when we are younger, there is a temptation to think we are immortal. That time doesn't matter much. There's this idea that there is always tomorrow. And you might forget, like I did, how many people actually got you to where you ended up and how long it actually took. When you're thirty, 20 years is reasonable, but when you are suddenly fifty or sixty years old, you don't have the luxury of time, so you need to really plan ahead. Being alone with money and big hobbies and good taste is a dangerous place to be.

So have a plan.

·······

AT THE END OF THE DAY, we are all in this game of building businesses because we can't think of anything better we'd rather be doing. Starting and building stuff is fun, keeps you "awake", and the uncertainty you live with every day is an adrenaline boost. Most people can't deal with it and quit early or give up. Some that stick through it all become the winners.

But if you get to the end game, you can be sure you are among a small percentage of humans who actually contribute value by creating something new or doing something different. That's a good thing. Being responsible for your team, your customers, and your investors is Big People stuff and taking on that responsibility weighs heavy on your soul every day. In fact, it's what you think about all the time, every day. There is no clocking in and out. Being useful is hard work.

So when you do get to the end game, and you get that payday "one-time hit", be sure to enjoy it. But make sure you have also thought about what's next and when. Don't go too far off-grid, because without a doubt, you still have a lot left in the tank and will need to hit the momentum button again. When you totally switch off, getting momentum primed again is super difficult; trust me, I've been there.

It's also probably going to be the first time in a long time you will have to actually sit down and think about things calmly; to really explore all the options. If you've been busy building a company 24/7 and solving problems for many years, you've not had time to think about some of the important things. I'm sure of that.

Your family will suddenly be there (that is, if they actually are still there), you will have time on your hands, there may be a lot of down-time soul searching, and maybe things you haven't wanted to address for years will pop up because you simply didn't have time. When you exit, you will find you have more time than you ever thought possible.

That can be scary.

THINGS TO THINK ABOUT

1. You need to think about what's next. If you see an exit or some liquidity event in the future, start taking stock of where you are in life.
2. Plan for the future; are you going to retire and if so, do you have enough? What's your burn rate and can you make adjustments.

3. Don't leave the game too long. Go on the massive holiday, rent a yacht and sail around and take time off, but get back before you get rusty and people forget you. Have the holiday and get back in your seat.
4. It's hard to flip the switch back and takes time. Have enough cash to start again if needs be.

CHAPTER 19

SELLING TACOS IN AFRICA

> *"Begin at the beginning," the King said, very gravely, "and go on till you come to the end: then stop."*
> —Lewis Carroll

IT'S TIME TO WRAP UP Tula's story, and I wish I could promise you a happier ending. But a happy ending is still possible—the story of Tula as an entrepreneur isn't over. The point is, it's never over. Startups come and go. Business ideas equally come and go, some better some not. Zillions of challenges along the way and loads of learning as you go.

Like a lot of entrepreneurs, Tula wanted to do everything at once and wouldn't give up his idea even when he knew it was over. He was mesmerised and more interested by all his "friends" on Facebook and likes on his web page than in the business. But these friends were not showing up on the spreadsheets.

In the end, there are only three ways to fund a losing business while hoping the tooth fairy will show up: more debt, more equity, or not paying suppliers or employees. I can't think of any other way. No one was going to lend him any more money, and he was not able to sell any more equity, so he was doing the only thing he could do. He wasn't paying anyone, and that only leads to tears and anger.

I explained that he had to list all his creditors, figure out the percentage of his debt that he owed to each of them, work out how much he could realistically pay them each month, and call them. If in fact he wanted to survive because he felt the business could manage its way forward. It's a daunting exercise, but one that would work. I'd done it myself years ago. Facing your demons and getting honest with creditors builds character.

His business model was like me trying to sell business plans or consulting services in New York. It's not going to happen. You need to sell tacos in Africa.

We talked more, and I remained firm that I wasn't going to lend him any money to get him out of trouble. "Meet with your uncle and put him on a payment plan. Write up a business plan and start over and start small," I told him. "Take with you all you've learned from your mistakes."

But he wanted those magic beans. He wanted someone to bail him out of his problems. I couldn't do that for him.

There are no magic beans. Only being ready, being in the right place, and taking a committed leap.

I know that's not what anyone wants to hear; it's not what he wanted to hear either, but it's true. Tula will only be successful when he faces his demons, takes a different path, and starts again. It's not a quick fix. Real success takes time. He will need to understand there are no short cuts.

·······

PERSONALLY, I THINK EVERYONE wants the same thing: to be happy, to control their lives, to live free from financial worries, and to have a career they love and are excited about. Those are all good things to want. You must find a way to be useful.

If you do what everyone else does and follow where every-one else goes, you will be like everyone else. You probably won't have those things that everyone wants. "Being like everyone else" is a crowded space.

The truth; real success or happiness is finding and doing something that makes you feel useful in life. If you find that state, then there's no stopping you. When you don't feel useful, it's time to stop or try something different.

In 1987, I had no foreseeable plan for my life. I had felt trapped in a job, a routine, doing the same thing and waiting for something different to happen. Then I lost my job. But noth-ing different was going to happen if I just waited. Eventually, I found a much better way. I took a leap of faith, and this path brought me to even better places than I could have imagined. I found a way to be useful. I solved problems.

A startup entrepreneur is like a modern-day explorer—going somewhere they have never been before. Like exploring Africa. That's what I've always considered myself to be. But to make that happen, I needed three things: first, *to take a leap of faith*, second *to have a vision and get good at narrating it*, and lastly, *to be willing to start small and do anything, anywhere.* Entrepreneurs make *"their"* thing, *"your"* thing. And when you do that, people follow you.

I remember how fun it was, and how time just seemed to fly by. Those eighteen years came and went quickly. I had gone on an adventure and built these businesses in uncertain market environments, in countries with different languages and cultures that I didn't understand. Like me, Eastern Europe was finding itself. Eastern Europe was Africa to me.

As I've written this book, I've had to look closely at myself in the mirror. What if I had to start all over again? I've done some amazing things, but that was yesterday. My office is full of pictures and press clippings, books, trophies, artwork, and fancy gizmos from my business days to remind me of who I am. But what about that line in the first chapter of this book? My claim that you could "drop me anywhere with $400, and I could start again." That idea is keeping me up at night these days.

....

WHEN I FIRST SET OUT to write this book, my title was just a metaphor about doing something different and following a different path than everyone else, prompted by meeting Tula. After many years of being off-grid, I felt I needed a download and wanted to write a book, mainly because I had time, and realised that maybe it could provide some valuable insights and help people; and to point out that business really is just one big adventure. I thought it would also be a good process for me to go through, forcing myself to retrace my steps in order to help me move forward.

But when I met with Tula and John-Paul and started a dialogue about Africa, it dawned on me that while the world may be large in size, it has become smaller via technology and therefore presents a far wider menu of opportunities – all the time, every minute. At the same time, it made me realise that you can't really chase them all and you need to stick to what you really know and in your own patch.

At the end of the day, with a lot of gas still in my tank and with a skill set that was put together over many years, I came to understand that chasing rabbits in Africa was a foolish notion, and that I needed to focus and build on what I knew. I had to Reboot.

For me, Africa is not so much a country or place, but rather an idea of high adventure. Starting any business is ultimately about venturing into the unknown and conquering doubt; both external and internal, and of course at the root, solving problems. The overwhelming joy of creating something brand new. It's about faith, commitment and persistence. Africa is the idea.

·······

IF I HAD TRIED to make a living writing business plans back in New York City in the 90s, I would never had made any money. Too many people doing that already. There are plenty of corporate finance boutiques and former execs and consultants that do that extremely well. And New York as we all know is a super competitive place. In Estonia in 1992, for a short period of time, I was one of the only guys doing that. For a time, I could charge what I wanted. It was an opportunity, albeit a small and short-lived one. But it gave me a start for other things that happened as if by total accident.

My trip to Estonia was an unchartered adventure into the unknown. I didn't speak the language, knew no one, and had very little money my pocket. Writing those business plans in Estonia was just the beginning of something (and I had no idea at the time) that would eventually become something else covering five emerging market countries.

Like all opportunities, there will be other people that see them too. Not just you. The upside is that most people will find excuses not to take that leap or they will make it overly complicated. I've learned that sometimes if you're too smart, you can find a million reasons why something won't work.

I recall trying to raise capital in the 90s in the UK and USA from investors for Central and Eastern Europe. Too small, too shallow, no liquidity, "isn't there a war?" not safe, no regulations, currency risk, low GDP . . . I could go on. Smart guys.

I developed at cap rates of 19%+ and later watched almost all of these same investors come piling in 2006-2008 at cap rates of 5%. Same smart guys. Sadly, it hardly ever changes; it just works like that.

If you spend too much time thinking about it and planning it out, waiting for the confirmation, the window will close pretty quickly. But for a while, those that step up and stick with it will have blue sky above them and be the only game in town, gaining a foothold that others will pay dearly for years later. Getting in and staying in makes all the difference.

There may be stench in the streets in Kumasi, but people are eating and even in poor countries and cities, distraction from everyday life is often a meal out. So why not Mexican food? There's no one else in the market, and it's a big market. In fact, there are opportunities like this across the globe and in your back yard.

Don't be fooled by the experts, all you need to do is just focus and start. Don't compare yourself with others. I am no business genius and there are plenty of people smarter who have far greater knowledge of real estate than I do. Most of them work for someone else. There's a huge difference between smarts and the comfort of a paycheque every month, and the dogged persistence and commitment of going on an adventure and spotting an opportunity in the bush.

I wasn't thinking about being in business on that square in Tallinn when I met Sergei. I was just out enjoying myself and admiring the architecture and the blond Estonian women. But as chance would have it, Sergei needed a business plan, and I helped him.

Sergei had asked me to write a plan for his new shop to present to a local bank, and I was off to the races. There were no local, expert financial consulting firms back then in these markets, and the new bank popping up wanted "western" business plans for their loan committees. I went from asking Sergei for $500 to upping my price each time and being able to charge up to $50,000 for new mandates. By the first summer I'd made a pile of money.

No one else could do that at that particular moment in time. It was *where I was* that made the difference. I solved a problem for a stranger, and that was the start of my business and solving problems ever since.

·······

WHEN YOU ARE THINKING ABOUT a sector to launch in, look for a market or opportunity where competition is lacking. Opening a quick service food business in one of London's hottest sectors means trying to muscle your way into a crowded market. There are thousands of guys doing the same thing. You are not going to solve anyone's problem by launching another fast food chain. All I can tell you is its thin margins and a lot of hard work. And most fail.

Look for that opportunity in the bush. For that Africa where little competition exists and where you are free to create and explore before everyone else catches up or catches on. It's a place or sector where there is little competition and pricing is still elastic. Writing my business plans in New York would have given me nothing, really. Writing plans in Eastern Europe after the fall of the Berlin Wall was easy.

When starting out, take time to consider the potential size of the addressable market, what the competition is doing, and how far they have gone. Consider what you bring to the table that is different—a new technology, service, or even a new marketing strategy. Think Red Bull. If you are to succeed, there must be something unique about what you are doing. Be prepared to keep changing it to stay ahead. Markets change quickly. Be ready and flexible. But always start with an edge.

That start, no matter how small, will open up other opportunities, and increase your network of contacts; for me, those business plans I wrote introduced me to the main lenders in the market. Those connections would become super valuable later on. Every dot connected whether I knew it or not. But I was there. I showed up.

THINGS TO THINK ABOUT

1. Nothing happens overnight, so be patient and stick with it.
2. Don't spend what you don't have.
3. Make sure you are doing something useful.
4. Stick with what you know; but look for uncontested space to do that in.

ACKNOWLEDGEMENTS

THE ONLY PERSON BRAVE ENOUGH to hold a mirror in front of me at critical moments is my wife, Marlene. And as difficult as it is sometimes to see the truth, sometimes it's good to have a brave and honest person holding up the mirror. I am also grateful for our son because he changed my world and made me a better and more responsible person. I thank all the people at Ober-Haus Real Estate, Hauser-Oberschneider, Schlossle Hotels, and Capfield for helping me build a few successful companies and accomplish the unthinkable in a moment in time; and for my colleagues at Hilltop and my partners at Round Hill Capital. Finally, I thank God every day for all the chances and "do overs" I get to try. Heaven knows I need the help!

ABOUT THE AUTHOR

Paul Oberschneider is an entrepreneur and property professional who has built multiple businesses across the emerging markets of Central and Eastern Europe after the fall of the Berlin Wall. In 1992, he helped start a bank credit department in an emerging market, then went on to build one of the largest fully integrated real estate companies across the CEE region under the Ober-Haus Real Estate brand; developing a portfolio of shopping centers and hypermarkets in Eastern Europe; hotels and residential developments. Paul retired at age 48, just before the financial crisis of 2008.

Recently, Paul founded a private equity real estate company in the UK that provides capital to residential property developers.

Paul's philosophy of business is simple: build a great team, stay focused, hustle, be useful and don't look down.

MY NOTES

Printed in Great Britain
by Amazon

58605347R00092